GREAT MISTAKES
IN EDUCATION POLICY

And How to Avoid Them in the Future

Ruth Lupton and Debra Hayes

First published in Great Britain in 2021 by

Policy Press, an imprint of Bristol University Press
University of Bristol
1-9 Old Park Hill
Bristol
BS2 8BB
UK
t: +44 (0)117 954 5940
e: bup-info@bristol.ac.uk

Details of international sales and distribution partners are available at
policy.bristoluniversitypress.co.uk

British Library Cataloguing in Publication Data
A catalogue record for this book is available from the British Library.

ISBN 978-1-4473-5245-7 paperback
ISBN 978-1-4473-5248-8 ePub
ISBN 978-1-4473-5246-4 ePdf

Cover design: Robin Hawes
Front cover image: iStock-96816531

Bristol University Press and Policy Press use environmentally
responsible print partners

Printed in Great Britain by CMP, Poole

Contents

List of tables and boxes

Tables

Boxes

List of tables and boxes

List of abbreviations

'A' Level	Advanced Level
AARE	Australian Association for Research in Education
ACARA	Australian Curriculum Assessment and Reporting Authority
AITSL	Australian Institute for Teaching and School Leadership
AP	Alternative provision (also analytic phonics)
ATAR	Australian Tertiary Admission Rank
CoC	City of Culture
CPD	Continuing professional development
DfE	Department for Education
DESE	Department of Education, Skills and Employment
DSP	Disadvantaged Schools Program
EAL	English as an Additional Language
EALD	English as an Additional Language or Dialect
EAZ	Education Action Zone
EEF	Education Endowment Foundation
EiC	Excellence in Cities
EPA	Education Priority Area
ERA	Education Reform Act
ESFA	Education and Skills Funding Agency
ESL	English as a Second Language
FSM	Free school meals
FTE	Full-time equivalent
GCSE	General Certificate of Secondary Education
GDP	Gross domestic product
GERM	Global Education Reform Movement
ICSEA	Index of Community and Socio-Educational Advantage
IPS	Independent public school

KS1	Key Stage 1
KS2	Key Stage 2
LEA	Local education authority
MCEECDYA	Ministerial Council for Education, Early Childhood Development and Youth Affairs
NAPLAN	National Assessment Program – Literacy and Numeracy
NASUWT	National Association of Schoolmasters Union of Women Teachers
NPD	National Pupil Database
NPM	New public management
NSW	New South Wales
NUT	National Union of Teachers
OECD	Organisation for Economic Co-operation and Development
Ofqual	Office of Qualifications and Examinations Regulation
Ofsted	Office for Standards in Education, Children's Services and Schools
OSA	Office of the Schools Adjudicator
PE	Physical education
PIRLS	Progress in International Reading Literacy Study
PISA	Programme for International Student Assessment
PP	Pupil Premium
PRU	Pupil Referral Unit
SAT	Standard Assessment Test
SEN	Special educational needs
SES	Socioeconomic status
SP	Synthetic phonics
STA	Standards and Testing Agency
TALIS	Teaching and Learning International Survey
TIMMS	Trends in International Mathematics and Science Study
TRA	Teaching Regulation Agency
UN	United Nations
USI	Unique student identifier

Notes on the authors

Ruth Lupton is Honorary Professor of Education at the University of Manchester. She researches, writes and teaches about poverty and inequality, particularly in relation to education and neighbourhoods. Previous books include *Poverty Street* (Policy Press, 2003), *Social Policy in a Cold Climate* (Policy Press, 2016, with Tania Burchardt et al) and *Responding to Poverty and Disadvantage in Schools* (Palgrave Macmillan, 2017, with Tamara Bibby and Carlo Raffo).

Debra Hayes is Professor of Education and Equity and Head of School at the Sydney School of Education and Social Work, University of Sydney. Formerly a secondary science teacher, her research explores how schooling practices benefit some groups of young people more than others. Previous books include *Education, Feminism, Social Justice: The Twentieth Century Life of Jean Blackburn* (Monash University Press, 2019, with Craig Campbell), and *Literacy, Leading and Learning: Beyond Pedagogies of Poverty* (Routledge, 2017, with Rob Hattam et al).

Acknowledgements

Many of the ideas for this book emerged during a series of walks on the moors of the North of England, during which we talked about the problems and possibilities for education in our two countries and shared understandings of how things have come to be as they are now and how they might change. We have had the privilege of being paid to think and to write, as full-time tenured academics. This book is our attempt to reach an audience beyond academia, and to make a contribution to our shared commitment to improving the education of young people, particularly those who rely most on schooling to enhance their opportunities for success, and to enrich their experiences of learning.

Like most worthwhile projects, it relies on the support, encouragement and prior work of others. We are grateful to all our colleagues whose work we reference in this book. Educational research as a field of knowledge is rich and diverse but vastly underappreciated. We hope that this book will encourage readers to develop a heightened appreciation of what the field has to offer in terms of current challenges and dilemmas in education.

Through the case studies in this book we have drawn on the work of many others who have generously permitted us to include their original research, and to shape it for our purpose to illustrate the conditions of schooling at the 'sharp end'.

Our special thanks go to Lyn Kerkham for her extensive literature searches, and her ongoing editorial assistance throughout the project. The book could not have been completed without her. We are also grateful to Rebecca Grant, who helped with some of the English research, Maralyn Parker for her feedback on our efforts to reach a larger audience, Bob Lingard for his timely and detailed feedback at the final stages of preparation of the manuscript, Carlo Raffo for supporting

Deb's Hallsworth Visiting Professorship at the University of Manchester in 2018/19, and the anonymous reviewers whose feedback helped us shape the proposal and finalise the work.

Our publisher, Policy Press, has remained patient and demanding in ways that have encouraged and enabled us to bring this project to completion in the face of shifting responsibilities and the disruptions due to the COVID-19 pandemic in the final months of preparing the manuscript. We are grateful for their enthusiasm and support for the project throughout.

Last but not least, we thank our families and close friends, who patiently supported and endured as we grappled with how to turn our idea into a reality, most especially Gaby Mason who saw it through from start to finish, and Nancy the Border Terrier, who accompanied us on those early walks. We are fortunate that our research and writing occurs in loving and secure spaces.

1

Introduction

Time to hit reset in education policy

This book is about the mistakes that have been made in education policy in England and Australia since the 1970s and how we can begin to put them right.

England and Australia are very different countries, with different education systems, histories and governance structures, but they have been following similar education policy trajectories. We argue that in many respects, these trajectories have made schooling in both England and Australia less rather than more able to meet the educational challenges our societies present.

In particular, as economic, social and spatial divisions have grown, the evidence is mounting that our education systems have become increasingly unfair in terms of access, opportunities, experiences and outcomes. And this is despite repeated political claims, over decades, that a major objective of education policies is to achieve greater equality of opportunity and greater social mobility based on more equal outcomes.

As we enter a new period of rapid technological, environmental, demographic and labour market change, super-charged by the COVID-19 pandemic and its disruptive effects, it is imperative we find ways to make our education systems work for all.

In this book, we argue that positive change *is* possible. There is no shortage of contemporary international examples that help point the way. But we need big policy changes, not policy 'tweaks'. Taken-for-granted assumptions and well-established structures must be challenged, and a new consensus built for substantial change.

This will require changes in the nature of policy debates and a greater willingness to set aside whims, prejudices and long-standing antagonisms. We need to reclaim some of the common ground that exists in collective aspirations for children's and young people's wellbeing and success. It will also require changes in policy processes and timescales, and in the ways that policy makers draw on research and practice expertise. But above all, it will require willingness to confront the mistakes of the past, regardless of who has made them. Transformational change will not be achieved without a strong shared understanding of what has gone wrong as well as what has gone right, and why decades of policy effort have not produced education systems that are effective and fair.

Seeing the wood, not just the trees

One of the biggest stumbling blocks to a new consensus is the sheer complexity of educational change and the huge volume of often contradictory information about almost every aspect of this process.

Consumers of the news media in both England and Australia are confronted with a continual barrage of claims and counter-claims about the state of their education systems. Results are up, or down, depending on whose interpretation you read. International rankings, or scores, are up (or down), in absolute terms or relative to other countries. More choice of schools is available, but most families have no choice. Behaviour is improving (or worsening). More (or fewer) children are passing tests, but tests are getting easier (or harder). Teachers are better qualified, but more teachers are leaving the profession. And so on. For policy makers, practitioners, and even 'experts' in education policy trying to take a long-term view of whether things have become better or worse, this is mind-bogglingly confusing, never mind for 'stakeholders' in education such as parents, teachers, school governors and young people themselves.

Assessing whether education has become better or worse *is* difficult. Education systems are complex, with multiple attributes, institutions and actors. They can be better in some respects and worse in others. For example, they can be better resourced but less efficient; less well-resourced but better equipped with pedagogies and curricula fitted to social and economic goals; better in terms of overall outcomes but worse in terms of inequalities between students; better in the short term but with weak foundations for sustainable success. Whether things are 'better' or 'worse' partly depends on your view of what education should be for and about.

Most people seem to agree that the economic purposes of education have moved centre stage in many education systems worldwide since the 1970s, although they do not agree whether this is a good thing. Even within this economic framing, tensions exist between those who argue for systems that, variously: promote basic skills in English and mathematics; emphasise science and technology; promote skills and attributes for networked, flexible and changing labour markets and 'portfolio careers'; and equip people with languages and understanding of global civilisations. Arguably tensions over the purposes of education have grown deeper as the demands on education systems to meet multiple goals have increased.

But these disputes are not the only reason it is difficult to work out what is going on.

The volume of research in education has expanded rapidly. A policy maker, educator or someone wanting information about a particular problem can 'find themselves confronted with a mountain of academic studies that are potentially relevant to the question' (Leigh, 2009, p 27). Evidence of policy effects is often mixed and sometimes contradictory, depending on what was looked at, who was asked, where and when. Faced by a cacophony of policy-relevant information, it is perhaps not surprising that policy makers sometimes over-rely on personal educational experiences and prejudices, or single studies or 'killer facts', or create false binaries (such as 'for or against higher standards', 'for or against all children learning to read') to build support for the policy programmes in which they believe.

Some have gone further. In the past decade, while there has been widespread agreement about the importance of research and evidence in education, battles have been fought about what kind of evidence matters, and who is considered an expert. Deep schisms seem to have opened up between different parts of the educational 'community': politicians, civil servants, school leaders, teachers and their unions, academics and researchers, professional associations, parents and governors. In England, former education secretary Michael Gove (2013) famously waged war on 'the blob' – education professionals and academics 'in thrall to the 1960s' who argued for 'progressive' approaches to education.

In this book, we try to get past the problem of 'not being able to see the wood for the trees'. We aim to present a clear and concise view of the great mistakes that have been made and what needs to change. Our view is based on a wide range of research evidence, qualitative and quantitative, and a balanced review and synopsis. We do not 'weaponise' research against itself. Educational research is incredibly diverse. As education academics skilled at navigating our way around its many bodies of research, we attempt to recognise and distinguish the strengths and limitations of different methodologies, and their various contributions to knowledge, while also calling out the misuse and over-claiming that often follows the phrase, 'research has shown' (Gibb, 2015a). We argue that, although there are still many unknowns, there *are* issues where the evidence *is* clear and which can be agreed upon.

It isn't all bad, but things need to change

So, what is the problem with education in England and Australia? Although the title of this book draws the reader to errors, mistakes and things that have gone wrong, we definitely do not claim that all is amiss with education in our two countries. On the contrary, much is good.

For reasons we discuss in detail at several points in this book, it is very difficult to know whether children and young people are learning more than they did in the past. In Australia, state and national test results would suggest that they are. In New South Wales (NSW), where the end-of-school external examinations are marked against a fixed standard, the proportion of students achieving the highest results (band six) in mathematics rose from 12 per cent in 2001 to more than 20 per cent in 2018 (Education Standards Authority, 2020). However, in international tests – the Organisation for Economic Co-operation and Development's

(OECD) Programme for International Student Assessment (PISA) – which are intended to assess how well students can apply knowledge learnt in school to the world beyond the classroom, Australia's results in mathematics have decreased steadily between 2000 and 2018, and in NSW the proportion of high achievers decreased (Thomson et al, 2019). These contrasting accounts of achievement suggest we need to focus on the substance of what is happening in education not just the top line figures, and we need to pay attention to how different groups are faring.

In many ways, the evidence suggests that over recent decades our schools have become much better places. More money is being spent on them, in real terms and as a percentage of national income or gross domestic product (GDP) (UNESCO, 2020). They have better buildings and equipment and less overcrowding, and teachers are better trained. Many would argue that they are also kinder, more respectful places, with an end to corporal punishment and greater recognition of the diversity of children and young people and their rights and voices. Fewer people are leaving school without basic education and more are going on to higher levels. In our daily work, too, with teachers, school leaders, students, parents, governors and educational policy makers, we are struck by the high quality of teaching and learning that goes on in our schools, and by the curiosity, excitement, resilience, hope and joy that characterises so many of the activities and interactions in an average school day in English and Australian schools, including those working in the toughest of circumstances.

However, these changes for the better cannot obscure the evidence that some major things have gone wrong. While education systems may be better in some respects, they are worse (or at least, insufficiently better) in others. Critically, we argue, they are worse in ways that threaten their fitness to respond to the challenges our societies face now and those they will face in the future.

In Chapters 3, 4 and 5, we point to three major problems:

- an overemphasis on test and examination success, leading to a narrower curriculum, diminished learning opportunities

and negative effects on well-being and well-becoming (Chapter 3);
- increasingly divided school systems that work for some but not others (Chapter 4);
- too much of teachers' time being spent on activities that fail to improve teaching and learning, meaning that although teachers are busier than ever they can make less of a difference (Chapter 5).

We argue these problems are limiting the capacity of schools to produce the skills and capabilities needed for 21st-century economies and societies, and making them in some respects less healthy, enjoyable and inspiring. They are also limiting schools' capacity to include all children and young people equally, combat inequalities in educational experiences and outcomes, reduce 'disadvantage gaps', and promote social mobility or however politicians want to express these kinds of equitable aims.

Education policies have often worked least well in the areas and schools where they need to work best – places that have historically been marginalised, or that have been most vulnerable in the transition from industrial to post-industrial economies, or in the face of international conflicts and transnational population movements. In these places where learning and teaching are most challenging and students and their families rely most on education systems, changes are having the most negative effects, thus reproducing or exacerbating existing divides between people and places.

In England, 'disadvantage gaps' in attainment (measured in national tests and examinations) between children and young people eligible for free school meals (FSM) and others have not narrowed significantly in the past 20 years, prompting the Education Policy Institute (2019) to observe that at the current rate of progress, it would take over 500 years for this gap to close completely at the end of secondary school. PISA data show a more positive 'over-time' story but the same wide socioeconomic gap (OECD, 2020b). Students from some minority ethnic groups (Bangladeshi and Pakistani) have made progress in recent years, while others (Indian and Chinese) have consistently been high achievers. White British students and Black Caribbean students from low socioeconomic status (SES) backgrounds continue to have relatively low attainment. Large regional differences persist (Lupton and Obolenskaya, 2020). In Australia, the performance gap related to SES in PISA 2018 was no smaller than in 2009 (Thomson et al, 2010, 2019). Across all domains measured by PISA there are consistent patterns of performance: students from metropolitan schools perform better than those in provincial schools, who in turn perform better than students in remote schools; students from higher socioeconomic backgrounds perform at a higher level than students from lower socioeconomic backgrounds; Indigenous students perform at a lower level than their non-Indigenous peers (Thomson et al, 2019). Similar geolocation differences are also apparent in the achievement results of Australian students reported in the National Assessment Program – Literacy and Numeracy (NAPLAN) (ACARA, 2019a) and the Trends in International Mathematics and Science Study (TIMMS) (Halsey, 2018). The extent of the gap between Indigenous and non-Indigenous students is further illustrated through the lower achievement of Aboriginal and Torres Strait Islander children in all states and territories in reading, writing and numeracy across all year levels tested on NAPLAN (Ford, 2013; Department of the Prime Minister and Cabinet, 2020).

These persistent inequalities, along with wider evidence from studies of schools and classrooms, prompted leading English and Australian professors Becky Francis and Martin Mills to argue that '[t]he current schooling system modelled across many OECD nations – including our own locations of England and Australia – is inherently damaging: damaging both in its institutional impact on children/young people and teachers as individuals, and in its fundamental perpetuation of social inequality' (Francis and Mills, 2012a, p 252).

If this is the case, and we think it is, then we are at a point where it is no longer possible to improve matters by carrying on broadly in the same direction with tweaks to existing policies. We are going to need a substantial and significant change of direction, realigning our education policies with our economic and social goals in new ways. But to do this, we must acknowledge the mistakes of the past and how they have brought us to where we are today.

Policy mistakes and their consequences

The policy mistakes we are interested in are those we call 'great mistakes'. In Chapters 6, 7, 8 and 9, we name and analyse four of these:

- turning to the market to improve standards in education (Chapter 6);
- orientating and managing the education system around the production of higher scores in academic tests (Chapter 7);
- over-prescribing teachers' work (Chapter 8); and
- failing to understand the causes of educational inequalities and how to address them (Chapter 9).

Each of these areas comprises, or has given rise to, multiple policies, programmes and schemes – for example, on curriculum and assessment, school system structures and funding, teacher professional development and professional standards. They have also produced specific policy technologies such as performance measures, inspections, incentives and rewards. However, by contrast with other books on policy mistakes, such as King and Crewe's (2014) *The Blunders of our Governments*, we do not focus on the detail of particular schemes, initiatives or decisions. Our focus, instead, is on big and persistent themes, directions and underlying assumptions in education policy that have, in combination, produced negative effects and failed in significant ways to address the challenges they were intended to overcome.

For the first two mistakes in particular, an enormous amount has already been written. There are thousands of books and papers on the subject of markets in schooling, choice, competition, 'high-stakes tests', performance measures and accountability. Plenty of others either assess the effects of different aspects of teacher 'quality', prescribe particular practices, bemoan changes to the teaching profession or evaluate specific programmes, policies, standards or regulations. Yet despite this abundance of knowledge, the policy juggernaut rolls along, and broadly along the same tracks. Partly this is because of the fifth great mistake, documented in Chapter 10: major problems with the ways in which knowledge is produced and used in policy making, including narrow understandings of the kind of evidence or methodologies that are needed, and a lack of evidence synthesis and/or policy memory.

We aim to show how these five mistakes have worked additively and over time to produce the changes in educational environments and practice that we document in the first half of the book. In Chapter 11, we give a single integrated example of 'a perfect storm' of policy mistakes, the case of synthetic phonics.

In this chapter, and throughout the book, we focus consistently on the impacts on areas, schools and students most vulnerable to the effects of economic and social change to show how these separate policies have worked together in places and on people.

Consensus and hope

Crucially, we position these great policy mistakes as the product of errors rather than malice.

This is not because we are uncritical of a lot of the decisions that have been made, or because we cannot see that many are the products of political and ideologically informed choices. We agree with many critical academic readings that describe how power and privilege are exercised through policy technologies and discourses to perpetuate inequality in the interests of the powerful.

However, in the main we aim to move on from a sociological critique of policy making to the kind of consensus building we believe is needed to build new and more effective approaches to policy making. We believe that our hope for better and fairer systems of schooling is widely shared. If the current situation is to change, we need to work with other people who have the will and capacity to change it, rather than to enter into a 'blame game'. And, as academics working in the field of education, we cannot stop at theorising and critiquing the system. We must work in applied and practical ways and be prepared to deal with the messy compromises of actual policy and its delivery: with prejudice and vested interests as well as good intent, and with the realities of limited knowledge, limited money and competing priorities.

So, through our 'great mistakes' label, we attempt to write a critical book that focuses on mistakes in order to build a positive proposal about what should happen and at the same time to try to re-establish common ground that provides a new starting point for debates about how to create a better, fairer schooling system. We attempt to speak to a broad range of people who have been affected by unsuccessful policies, and to mobilise the intellectual and economic wealth of our nations towards better and fairer systems of education. We argue for a new foundation for education policy based on a reckoning of past policies and practices informed by a clear-headed analysis of where these approaches have taken us. And, as the book's subtitle says, we aim to help avoid further policy mistakes in education in the future.

In a book of this length, dealing with two countries, it cannot be our aspiration to set out new policy manifestos with detailed policy prescriptions. But we do hope to convince readers that the education policy systems in our two countries need not languish in a state of policy stasis, seemingly stuck in a rut of ineffective efforts over how to transform education for the better. We hope to show that problems can be seen in different ways, using wider sources of evidence, and that if we look more broadly and more honestly at what has happened in the past, and the alternatives that are emerging in other parts of the world, we can collectively get a better grip on the complex nature of educational problems and therefore their solutions.

In Chapter 12 we offer a blueprint for policy making in the future and propose some broad principles of educational reform that could both put right the mistakes of the past and better address the needs of the present and future. No generation in the past has been handed the legacy of a world with severely damaged ecosystems and unstable climatic conditions, at the same time as being faced with a pandemic-induced global economic shock of huge proportions and rapidly accelerating economic transformation due to the advance of artificial intelligence, which will likely have lasting effects on labour conditions and the way we live our lives. Education will be changed by these conditions and can shape their evolution. Societies around the world must now incorporate lessons learnt during the COVID-19 crisis about the critical role of education in preparing citizens to understand complex modelling and to respond collectively to a global health emergency and its economic impacts. The role of schools and of teachers has also been under intense scrutiny and, in some instances, their work is being valued and understood in new ways as parents around the globe deal with the challenge of supporting their children to learn at home.

In this context, small additive reforms that keep a broken system creaking along are a waste of money, a denial of the facts, and a failed response to young people who will bear the responsibility of finding solutions to the world's many problems. As always, the stakes are highest for those who rely most on schooling to secure their future opportunities for work and well-being. It is time for bolder and better-informed solutions.

2

Setting the scene

School systems in England and Australia

Many people reading this book will know a lot about education in England or in Australia, but perhaps not about both. This chapter sets the scene.

In an era of international 'policy borrowing' and 'policy convergence' (Ball, 1999, 2019; Sahlberg, 2015), there are many similarities between their education policies. We argue that politicians in both countries have made the same wrong turns and are dealing with some of the same consequences. Yet there are important differences in the structures and organisation of the systems themselves. These enable, or constrain, particular policy choices, creating so-called 'path dependencies' in the policy process, and they mean that policies play out in different ways. So, we start by setting out some of the essential characteristics of these education policy landscapes.[1]

A fundamental issue is who makes decisions about schooling. England[2] has a highly centralised system. Central government, in the form of the Department for Education (DfE), sets teachers' pay scales and professional standards. Systems of assessment and qualification are national, as is the curriculum, and school inspection, although these functions are managed by semi-independent organisations (see Table 2.1). Until relatively recently, there was also a strong role for local education authorities (LEAs). This has been much reduced by the creation of autonomous schools that all report to the DfE. The funding system is now also based on a single national formula. So, the system is simultaneously becoming more centralised and more

Table 2.1: Key organisations in the English and Australian school systems, c. 2020

Abbreviation	Organisation(s)	Role(s)
England		
DfE	Department for Education	Overall responsibility for school system, policy and funding. Sets curriculum policy and standards for teachers.
Ofsted	Office for Standards in Education, Children's Services and Schools	Inspects schools.
Ofqual	Office of Qualifications and Examinations Regulation	Regulates qualifications and examinations offered by independent bodies.
STA	Standards and Testing Agency	Develops and delivers national assessments in primary phase.
TRA	Teaching Regulation Agency	Regulates the teaching profession.
ESFA	Education and Skills Funding Agency	Administers government funding to schools.
LEAs	Local education authorities	Plan school places, ensure everyone has an education, provide school transport, employ teachers and provide other functions (buildings, admissions) for community schools.
OSA	Office of the Schools Adjudicator	Rules on disputes over school admissions.
Australia		
Various abbreviations	Education systems of the six states and two territories	Each administers the education system in its jurisdiction.
DESE	Department of Education, Skills and Employment	Australian government department that distributes funds from national taxes to state and territory governments.
AITSL	Australian Institute for Teaching and School Leadership	A wholly owned company funded by the Commonwealth of Australia responsible for developing national standards for educators and a career framework for teachers and leaders.
ACARA	Australian Curriculum Assessment and Reporting Authority	An independent statutory authority responsible for developing the national curriculum framework, and national assessment and public reporting strategy.
MCEECDYA	Ministerial Council for Education, Early Childhood Development and Youth Affairs	Intergovernmental policy council comprised of state, territory, Australian government and New Zealand ministers with responsibility for the portfolios of school education, early childhood development and youth affairs.

14

subject to hyper-local variation as schools can make more of their own decisions.

The Commonwealth of Australia is a federal system of government. The central – or national – government has no specific constitutional responsibility for school education. The six state and two territory governments have historically had responsibility for administration of government schools; development and delivery of curricula; and the regulatory conditions to ensure quality standards across all schools (including non-government schools). However, the constitution allows the national government to provide specific-purpose payments that enable central influence over areas that the states administer. In recent times, these powers have been activated in ways that have greatly extended the influence of the national government over education. Since 2008, Australia has progressively adopted elements of a national assessment programme, a national curriculum, and national professional standards for teachers that articulate with state-based mechanisms. Unlike in England, there is no tradition of elected local (sub-state or territory) education authorities.

Other key differences relate to the types of schools, and who runs and pays for them. In England, the vast majority of children and young people are educated in state schools wholly funded by the government. Most are mainstream schools, but there are also special schools for children with additional needs and/or disabilities, and Pupil Referral Units (PRUs) and other alternative provision for those excluded from mainstream schools. This state school sector is diverse, including community schools run by LEAs, faith schools run by diocesan authorities, foundation schools, academies and free schools (the latter three all run by not-for-profit trusts and having varying freedoms over admissions, governance, curriculum and other matters). Most state schools are comprehensive in intake but some (grammar schools) are academically selective. Around 7 per cent of pupils are educated outside the state sector, attending fee-paying independent schools that do not receive public funding and are in most ways independent of government regulations. Many, but not all, of these independent schools are academically selective and some are single-sex or have a religious orientation.

In Australia, all schools receive government funding if they adhere to a range of regulatory requirements related to the national curriculum, and to assessment and reporting frameworks. Government schools provide for around two thirds of students and are administered by state or territory departments. The remainder of schools are either governed by a system authority other than a state or territory department, such as Catholic schools run by dioceses, or they are independent schools that operate autonomously and are separately accountable to their parent and school communities. The independent sector includes low to high fee-paying schools that are mostly faith-based. The federal government has provided funding since 2014 for government schools to become independent public schools, similar to those that have existed for some time in Western Australia with increased local governance, and financial flexibility (including staffing), but otherwise these schools remain part of their state system. Most schools across all sectors are comprehensive in intake but some are academically selective or selective according to other criteria, such as those that have specialist programmes in music, mathematics and science, or languages. Schools offering special education are located across all school systems. There is also a growing number of alternative or flexi-schools, some of which are administered and funded by not-for-profit organisations, that provide alternative learning choices for young people who, for a variety of reasons, are unable to access and attend other schools or who seek more flexible learning arrangements. These schools are called special assistance schools in the independent sector and are generally classified as behaviour schools in the state sector.

These differences mean that issues of access (who goes where) and resource allocation (which schools get what) play out differently in the two countries. They also mean that the processes by which policy decisions are made and the ways that high-level decisions are translated into practice in schools and classrooms are different both between and within the two countries. This is important in understanding the policy mistakes we describe, as well as thinking about how we could put them right.

Table 2.2: At a glance: school systems in England and Australia

	England	Australia
Wholly state-funded schools	**Maintained or 'state' schools (93.4%)** • Primary schools • Comprehensive secondary schools • Selective secondary (grammar) schools • Special schools • PRUs and other alternative provision Include community schools, voluntary aided and controlled faith schools, and academies and free schools, with different levels of non-state involvement and autonomy.	**Government schools (65.7%)** • K-6 primary schools, some including selective streams • Comprehensive secondary schools, some including selective streams • Selective secondary schools • Special schools – supporting disability, behaviour, or mental health issues • Behaviour schools • Independent state schools Include only schools run by state and territory departments, not diocesan schools or schools run by business groups, trusts or charities with various degrees of autonomy/state regulation.
Non-government schools – partly state-funded	**None**	**Systemic schools**, mainly Catholic schools run by dioceses (19.5%) **Independent schools** governed at the school level (14.8%) Non-government schools include a range of school types including those that are academically selective, special schools, and special assistance schools.
Private schools – no state funding	**Independent schools (6.6%)** Diverse fee-paying sector including elite academically selective schools, faith-based schools, other lower fee-paying schools serving particular interests, and some special schools.	

Social and spatial divisions

Schools do not exist in an educational bubble. As has been abundantly clear during the COVID-19 pandemic, they have to respond to challenges and changes in the economy and society, not least children's different and inequitable home circumstances and resources. A key argument of this book is that the provision of education in England and Australia has not responded adequately to the major issue of our time: widening and deepening social and spatial divisions.

England and Australia are both very rich countries. On the measure of household disposable income or the income of households after taxes and in-kind transfers (such as free healthcare), Australia ranks as the fifth richest OECD country, after the US, Luxembourg, Switzerland and Germany. The UK[3] ranks 15th. Both are highly unequal – England more so, as we shall show. Yet the share of people who live in relative income poverty is higher in Australia than on average in OECD countries, while in Great Britain it is lower, according to the OECD Income distribution and Poverty Database (Sila and Dugain, 2019a). And in common with many other advanced industrial nations, the extent of inequality and poverty has become perhaps *the* major political issue in recent times, as decades of economic growth have not produced more equally shared prosperity (Wilkinson and Pickett, 2009; Stiglitz, 2013; Piketty, 2014; Dorling, 2018).

In England, the problem is not *rising* inequality but stubbornly high levels. Since the 1980s, the UK has had fairly stable and high income inequality by international standards (Obolenskaya and Hills, 2019). In 2018, on the most common measure of income inequality – the Gini coefficient – it had the sixth highest level of income inequality of the 37 OECD countries. Patterns of spatial and social inequalities have, however, evolved in recent decades. One marked trend is the growing prosperity of London compared with other cities and regions (Obolenskaya et al, 2016; UK2070 Commission, 2020). The transition from an industrial to a post-industrial knowledge economy has also favoured major cities over older industrial towns (Beatty and Fothergill, 2018) and coastal towns formerly dependent on tourism, fishing and associated industries (House of Lords Select Committee on Regenerating Seaside Towns and Communities, 2019). But poverty and labour market precarity is not limited to ex-industrial towns. Major cities, including London, with their high costs of housing and living and strong representation of low-paid and precarious sectors (such as hospitality, retail and care), have continuing high rates of poverty and inequality, as the new economy creates divisions within cities as well as between them.

Australia is also dealing with increasing social and spatial divisions. Here too, long-standing patterns of inequality remain. In 2018, in terms of the Gini coefficient, it had the 14th highest level of income inequality of the 37 OECD countries. There are differences in household incomes from major cities to remote areas, and between states. In the past 20 years, the mining boom has contributed to a fast rise in incomes in Western Australia and some remote areas, but the majority of people live in major cities, and more than half live in the two most populous states of NSW and Victoria (Sila and Dugain, 2019b). The highest rates of poverty are outside the major cities, but since Australia is highly urbanised, the highest number of people living in poverty are located in major cities. Indigenous Australians are almost twice as likely to be poor than the rest of the population, and this gap is widening (Sila and Dugain, 2019a). Putting aside the unfolding economic impact of the 2020 pandemic, the period since 1991 has for the most part been a period of sustained economic growth in Australia (Battellino, 2010). But as in England, growth has been accompanied by greater shifts in the fortunes of different sectors and places. Decline in mining and manufacturing industries has created 'rust belt' areas in outer-rim suburbs of major cities and regional, large, single-industry towns. Growth in the services sector has resulted in four out of every five Australians being employed in this industry (Department of Foreign Affairs and Trade, 2020). Employment has become more flexible and precarious. The share of non-standard workers, comprising self-employed people, part-timers, casual workers and those on fixed-term contracts, is high at around 44 per cent, compared with the OECD average of one third (OECD, 2018).

The challenge for education policy

We argue that while politicians have been concerned with raising educational standards across the board, they have failed to pay enough attention to the different educational contexts experienced by children and young people and arising from social and spatial divisions, and how to make education equitable in these circumstances.

Much of our previous work (Hayes et al, 2005, 2017; Lupton, 2011; Thomson and Lupton, 2017) has analysed the changing conditions in areas characterised by high levels of poverty and also often high levels of difference. We have documented the implications for day-to-day life in schools and classrooms and for the practice of school leaders and teachers of working in these challenging contexts. We have argued that it is simultaneously more difficult and more important to get education right in such places.

It is more difficult to get education right in challenging contexts because economic and social difficulties put pressure on children, young people and their families and on schools as organisations. Poverty and lack of economic opportunity create barriers to learning and affect educational identities, hopes and expectations (Lamb et al, 2015; Skattebol et al, 2015). This is particularly so in England's ex-mining, ex-industrial and coastal areas (Bright, 2011; Reid and Westergaard, 2017; McDowell and Bonner-Thompson, 2020), and Australia's rust-belt and rural areas (Thomson, 2002; Hayes et al, 2017). Schools are required to respond to intense challenges: child poverty, stress, mental and physical health problems, insecurity and crime. Such challenges are not limited to those emerging from within nations. Education in the 21st century is responding to the highest number of forced displacements of all time – roughly half of all refugees are under 18 (UNHCR, 2020). Schools in some of England's and Australia's urban areas are dealing not just with domestic poverty, but also with the needs of young people studying in unfamiliar cultures and languages and coping with the effects of trauma and multiple losses (Hattam and Every, 2010; Block et al, 2014). Schools in the least advantaged areas also often manage with fewer resources. Consequently, intake pressures must be managed by weaker schooling organisations than those in more stable or advantaged settings due to difficulties with teacher recruitment and retention, declining enrolments and income, poor local reputations and/or high levels of pressure and uncertainty over their future. Increasingly, studies of school effectiveness and school improvement have pointed to the importance of context not just for individual students and their outcomes but for schools and the support and resources they need to improve as organisations (McNally, 2015).

It is also more important that education works really well in areas of social and economic pressure because it is there that students and families rely more on schooling to supplement the economic, social and cultural capital that their counterparts in better-off areas enjoy. Benefits available to better-off students include having family members who have attended university; access to household books and digital literacies, internet connectivity and related devices; family outings that enrich the formal (limited) knowledge of schooling; opportunities to participate in extra-curricular activities and classes; confidence in their future well-being and prosperity; visible pathways to labour market success; and levels of material security or savings that enable risky strategies such as spending time on studying subjects that are interesting but not necessarily likely to contribute to post-school opportunities (Lareau, 2011; Skattebol and Hayes, 2016; Reay, 2017).

So designing education policies that work really well for the least advantaged learners and in the least advantaged places is difficult, but it is essential if all children and young people are to get 'a fair go' and if education systems are going to have a levelling effect, and contribute to increased social mobility and reduced inequality in future generations. Arguably this is the real test of whether education policies are performing equitably and well.

Schools 'at the sharp end'

As we proceed through this book, setting out the problems of current arrangements as we see them, and then the mistakes that have contributed to them, we keep a focus on the kinds of schools in which it is most imperative that education works fairly and well, and where it is most difficult to pull this off –

Box 2.1: Introduction to English cases

Farrell High School is a large, inner-urban comprehensive high school in the north of England. The research we draw on (Firth et al, 2014) was conducted by a group of research active senior leaders in the school – Ben Firth, Victoria Melia, Dave Bergan and Lisa Whitby – which makes for a rare contribution by teachers to the academic literature. Their location in the school affords a deep understanding of local conditions. Farrell High School was graded a 'failing' school by Ofsted in 2009 and placed in special measures. The case highlights the confounding and perverse potential of performance measures to cap student achievement.

Parkside Academy is also an inner-urban high school in a northern city, located in an area of extreme social disadvantage. The current school was created in the early 2000s as part of the academies programme, which closed down inner-city secondary schools seen to be 'failing' and replaced them with independent, state-funded schools with sponsors. However, the Ofsted interpretation of the school that Parkside replaced was relatively positive. Parkside forms a case study of school autonomy by Maija Salokangas and Mel Ainscow (2018).

Six **coastal academy secondary schools** make up a case set in seaside towns/cities in England. All are in geographically remote areas of long-standing structural deprivation and cultural isolation. The schools serve mainly White working-class communities that have experienced a decline of industry, combined with poor infrastructure and local economies marked by short-term and low-paid jobs. This case draws on a body of research conducted since 2010 by Tanya Ovenden-Hope and Rowena Passy that identifies challenges to school improvement for such schools (Ovenden-Hope and Passy, 2015; Passy and Ovenden-Hope, 2017, 2020) and has conceptualised the limited access to resources for school improvement due to place-based 'educational isolation' (Ovenden-Hope and Passy, 2019).

Dreamfields is an inner-urban high school where the researcher, Christy Kulz (2017), was once a teacher. The school is an academy that replaced a 'failing school'. Residents of the borough and the children at the school come from a mix of social and economic backgrounds – 'poverty and gentrification coexist' (Kulz, 2017, p 1). The apparent success of the school's authoritarian approach has attracted attention. The case illustrates the policy mistakes we claim have produced and legitimised its approaches, and that these are at odds with so much of what we have come to understand as quality teaching and learning.

The case of four **English urban primary schools** describes the efforts of their leaders to support students to become good readers through reading for pleasure and sustained engagement in reading. Using a multiple case study design, Amelia Hempel-Jorgensen, Teresa Cremin, Diane Harris and Liz Chamberlain (2018) investigated the potential of reading for pleasure to encourage children's volition and social interaction as readers.

Box 2.2: Introduction to Australian cases

The case of six **Queensland rural primary schools** forms part of a three-year project into teachers' work and learning practices in a state where there was strong policy support for national testing after schools there had performed relatively poorly in the first NAPLAN tests in 2008. Ian Hardy's (2015) sustained analysis of how teachers and school-based administrators navigate the processes of accountability and standardisation provides an opportunity to assess the impact of this context on teachers' work and learning. The six schools reflect a mix of geographic, demographic and socioeconomic diversity. Three of the schools match our classification of schools at 'the sharp end'.

Northwest College is a secondary school situated in a low-income, working-class area in an outer suburb of Melbourne where Jen Jackson and Stephen Lamb (2016) conducted their research into the educational marketplace. Its public profile on the MySchool website 'is liberally adorned with the red pixels that signify educational failure' (Jackson and Lamb, 2016, p 5). Northwest College makes extensive use of vocational education options. However, despite these options, in the years 2009–13 between 12 and 16 per cent of Northwest College school completers left without a school-leaving certificate.

City Campus is the senior campus of Federation High School. Federation City has several suburbs ranked among the most disadvantaged communities in regional Australia. Once dominated by mining, agriculture and manufacturing, the economy is now more oriented towards tertiary industries, including education. Research conducted by Peter McInerney and John Smyth (2014) incorporates young people's narratives of socioeconomic disadvantage and the educational opportunities and constraints they experienced in the region. City Campus provides a range of academic and vocational subjects for Year 11 and 12 students, leading to accredited certificates of education.

The impact of the decline in Australia's manufacturing industry on outer-rim suburbs in large cities is the backdrop for the **Northern primary schools** case. These government schools in Adelaide were part of a three-year study into leadership and pedagogical practices that we conducted with Rob Hattam, Barbara Comber, Lyn Kerkham and Pat Thomson during the period 2012–15 (Hayes et al, 2017). The schools were chosen because their results stood out in a positive way compared with schools operating in similar contexts.

The case of **Waterwell Primary School** is drawn from Barbara Comber's (2012) study of the reorganisation of teachers' work, in particular their teaching of literacy, after one year of national testing in Australia. Comber adopted an institutional ethnography approach, working in one primary school to study the 'micro practices of actual people' who are doing the 'substantive on-the-ground work of policy reform' (2012, p 122).

Table 2.3: Summary of case studies

England

School pseudonym	Type/location and features at the time of each study
Farrell High School (Firth et al, 2014)	• Large urban comprehensive high school, north of England.
	• Students eligible for FSM 40% (national average 26.7%); minority ethnic student population 45.3% (national average 23.5%); students with English as an Additional Language (EAL) 20.8% (national average 13%); social deprivation indicator 0.28% (national average 0.21%).
Parkside Academy (Salokangas and Ainscow, 2018)	• Inner-urban high school in northern city with an ethnically diverse student population – African Caribbean and Black African students comprise the largest groups, others include those from Indian, Pakistani and Chinese backgrounds.
	• The majority of students came from low-income families, and about 50% from one-parent families, foster homes or households shared with other family members.
Coastal academy secondary schools (Passy and Ovenden-Hope, 2020)	• Six state-funded, sponsored academy secondary schools in seaside towns/cities in different regions of England.
	• Local communities predominantly White working-class. All had high numbers of pupils eligible for pupil premium (PP) funding and high or medium-to-high levels of pupils with special educational needs (SEN) and/or disabilities.
Dreamfields (Kulz, 2017)	• Academy in a mixed area of a large English city where gentrification has long been underway.
	• 40% of students eligible for FSM; more than 80% of students come from ethnic minority backgrounds, with Black African, Black Caribbean, Turkish, Bangladeshi and Indian students comprising the largest groups.
English urban primary schools (Hempel-Jorgensen et al, 2018)	• Located in different parts of England where reading for pleasure was reported to be valued by school leaders.
	• All schools had above-average (17%) levels of students eligible for FSM and of differing ethnic compositions.

(continued)

Table 2.3: Summary of case studies (continued)

Australia

School pseudonym	Type/location and features at the time of each study
Northwest College (Jackson and Lamb, 2016)	• Located in a low-income, working-class area in an outer suburb of a large city. Through processes of residualisation, the students have been increasingly drawn from disadvantaged communities.
City Campus (McInerney and Smyth, 2014)	• Secondary school in a large regional centre in south-eastern Australia that lacks the ethnic diversity of major cities and is highly stratified along socioeconomic lines. Several suburbs have been ranked among the most disadvantaged communities in regional Australia.
Northern primary schools (Hayes et al, 2017)	• Cluster of three primary schools in outer rim of Adelaide's northern suburbs. • Mainly white working-class neighbourhoods, with relatively large numbers of children from Aboriginal families, and growing cultural diversity. • 51%–81% of students approved for financial assistance; 9%–24% with English as an Additional Language or Dialect (EALD); 53%–68% Aboriginal; 3%–24% with SES.
Queensland rural primary school (Hardy, 2015)	• A diverse mix of schools including a school located in a regional and remote area, serving a predominantly Indigenous community; a school in a low SES community in a regional coastal city, and; a school located on the western edge of a greater urban area serving a community characterised by inter-generational poverty.
Waterwell Primary School (Comber, 2012)	• Low SES community that is linguistically and culturally diverse in suburban Adelaide, South Australia. • 60% of students approved for financial assistance; 13% from Aboriginal or Torres Strait Islander communities; 72% with English as a Second Language (ESL).

schools in places that have been 'at the sharp end' of increasing social and spatial divisions. In order to illustrate the conditions in these schools, particularly the challenges associated with learning, teaching and leading in them, we insert case studies in relevant places in Chapters 3 to 9 that demonstrate the impact of educational policies on a selection of English and Australian schools. In so doing, we also address the problem that evidence from such schools is often invisible. Schools in the most challenging circumstances do come to public attention from time to time, often to be 'named and shamed' for poor examination results or because of organisational crises, takeovers or closures. But their ongoing struggles and successes are routinely poorly documented or understood, and their unusual challenges can be smoothed out in area or system-wide data.

The cases selected are from peer-reviewed and academic research published between 2014 and 2019, and found through a search of educational databases using terms related to disadvantage, poverty and marginalisation, as well as school disaffection, 'at-risk' students, and disengagement. The studies generally utilised artefacts, interviews and observations over time, and some were part of larger research projects. In relation to classroom practice, they complement large-scale surveys by detailing what teachers do in their classrooms, and are thus particularly helpful for understanding the nature and influences on their classroom practices.

Brief details of the cases are provided in Boxes 2.1 and 2.2. The cases reappear throughout the book as we illustrate the impact of policy mistakes. As will become apparent, the evidence suggests that they have been 'on the sharp end' of education policy decisions, not just of social and spatial divisions. They illustrate what has gone wrong in education policy, why we need to change it, and that the resources and hope exist in order to do so.

We have adopted the fictional names assigned to the schools in the original research or created our own pseudonyms. While the schools are all real, their names are not.

Notes

[1]	Simply for reasons of manageability, this book covers schools, not the wider education system such as pre-school, vocational education and training in colleges and with employers, and higher education. A case can be made that the segmentation of the system into these parts is a mistake in itself, but that is for another book.

[2]	Since 1999 education has been a devolved responsibility, with very different policies in England, Wales, Scotland and Northern Ireland. Here we focus just on England.

[3]	OECD statistics report on the UK as a whole, not England. England has about 85 per cent of the UK's population.

3

Tests, tests, tests

This chapter is the first of three in which we set out the problems manifest in our current schooling systems. We put the biggest problem first – schools are becoming dominated by tests, in ways that are detrimental to children and young people and limit education rather than improving it.

In England, children do external tests from their first year of schooling. They take a phonics check in Year 1, Standard Assessment Tests (SATs) for English and maths at the end of Year 2 and again in Year 6, the General Certificate of Secondary Education (GCSE) or equivalent examinations at the end of Year 11, and Advanced ('A') Levels or equivalent at the end of Year 13. There are also standard teacher assessments at the end of the Foundation Stage (age about five).

In Australia, assessment regimes vary across state jurisdictions. However, in the earlier grades (3, 5, 7, and 9) ACARA conducts national assessments in literacy and numeracy through NAPLAN. The Year 12 end-of-school record of achievement is determined by each jurisdiction and may include a range of academic and vocational subjects assessed through a variety of means including examinations, performance tasks and portfolios. On completion of schooling, eligible students may also receive an Australian Tertiary Admission Rank (ATAR), which ranks them relative to others in their state or territory for university admission purposes.

The ways in which these assessment regimes shape the practice of teachers' and children's experiences of school has been the subject of numerous academic studies, enquiries and reviews by parliamentary committees, independent review bodies, teacher unions and others. They come to the same conclusions. Tests have many valid and valuable purposes but the situation is out of balance. Tests are dominating school life and creating a narrower curriculum, shallower learning, and more anxiety and unhappiness. They tend to exacerbate inequalities rather than reduce them. And, worryingly, in relation to the challenges outlined in Chapter 2, they tend to have the most pronounced effects in less advantaged schools and communities.

Narrower and shallower

In 2017, England's Chief Inspector of Schools (Head of Ofsted), Amanda Spielman, used a major speech to remind the educational establishment not to lose sight of the "substance of education" – in her words "broadening minds, enriching communities and advancing civilisation" (Spielman, 2017) – through over-focusing on tests.

Spielman pointed to two problems caused by the dominance of tests. One was the structure of the curriculum overall. Some primary schools, she said, were starting practice papers for the Key Stage 2 (KS2) SATs two years early, meaning that from Year 4 they would be increasingly focusing on English and maths. Some were 'effectively suspending Year 6 to focus exclusively on SATs' (Spielman, 2018). Some secondary schools were starting GCSE exam preparation in Year 9 (rather than Year 10 as has traditionally been the case), and sometimes as early as Year 7. So a 'broad and rich curriculum' was being sacrificed to test success in a narrow range of subjects. The other problem was what was happening in individual subject lessons, where active test preparation was taking over from actual learning. Spielman cited lessons where 'everything is about the exam and where teaching the mark schemes has a bigger place than teaching history' and schools which were 'forcing pupils ... to retake reading comprehension papers, with the purpose of boosting the schools' results, not their pupils' abilities to read' (Spielman, 2018).

Given her position at the head of an organisation that has contributed to English schools focusing on testing, Amanda Spielman's observations are particularly noteworthy. But what she describes is only the tip of an iceberg of evidence that a narrower curriculum and shallower learning are driven by the dominance of tests.

Over ten years ago, a House of Commons inquiry into testing and assessment (House of Commons Children, Schools and Families Committee, 2008), found that the curriculum had narrowed, and 'a focus on test results compromises teachers' creativity in the classroom and children's access to a balanced curriculum' (p 3). Other features of the current system were shallow learning, pupil stress and demotivation, and a disproportionate focus of resources on the borderline of targets. A year later, the Cambridge Primary Review reported its findings. This huge review analysed evidence from over 1,000 written submissions, 200 meetings and 28 surveys of published research evaluating over 3,000 published sources. From this vast exercise, the '*one thing* the Review's witnesses, submissions and research evidence are agreed on is that national tests and tables are narrowing the curriculum, [and] limiting children's learning' (Hofkins and Northen, 2009, p 30) (emphasis added).

In 2015, the National Union of Teachers (NUT) commissioned Professor Merryn Hutchings to carry out an independent study based on an online survey of nearly 8,000 teachers, which was entitled *Exam Factories*. It found overwhelming evidence of curriculum narrowing, with 97 per cent of teachers agreeing that there had been an increased focus on maths and English teaching. In primary schools, many teachers reported that the amount of time spent on maths and English in Year 6 was such that other curriculum areas (such as music, art, design and technology, and topic work) were taught less, or not at all. Around 90 per cent of teachers in all phases said that the focus on academic targets was reducing opportunities for creative, investigative and practical activities. As one said:

> Everything is about test results; if it isn't relevant to a test then it is not seen as a priority. This puts too much pressure on pupils, puts too much emphasis on academic subjects and creates a dull, repetitive curriculum that has no creativity. It is like a factory production line chugging out identical little robots

with no imagination, already labelled as failures if they haven't achieved the right level on a test. (Primary teacher, cited in Hutchings, 2015, p 10)

Box 3.1: The damaging effects of testing in four English primary schools

The case of four English urban primary schools provides some insight into the effects of overemphasising testing in communities with high levels of poverty and difference, the kinds of schools where classroom practices tend to be stripped down to emphasise transmission of knowledge and skill development, which has long been associated with 'pedagogies of poverty' (Haberman, 1991). Hempel-Jorgensen and colleagues (2018) selected these schools because reading for pleasure was expressly valued by school leaders. However, despite this, classroom practices in the participating schools reflected proficiency outcomes – students' technical abilities with aspects of reading were displayed in classrooms and teachers were more likely to perform administrative tasks during independent reading times instead of modelling the practice of reading. In three of the schools, approaches to reading for pleasure, such as encouraging children to talk about texts and sustained engagement in reading, were generally not supported or encouraged. The study shows the difficulties in supporting young people to become actively engaged in learning and in meaning-making activities in contexts where pedagogies of poverty are prevalent. Instead, they are more likely to be required to comply with learning activities that involve limited opportunities for thinking deeply, creatively or critically.

Because the Australian experience of national tests is more recent, there are fewer studies on the effects of these tests than in England, but there are some very substantial ones nonetheless. There have also been two separate inquiries of the Senate Employment, Education and Training References Committee (2010, 2014). The first was into the administration and reporting of NAPLAN testing and the second into the matter of the effectiveness of NAPLAN. The latter noted a number of negative unintended consequences such as a 'narrowing of the curriculum or "teaching to the test"; the creation of a NAPLAN preparation industry which compounds the perception that NAPLAN is a "high-stakes" test; and adverse or negative impacts on students' (Senate Employment, Education and Training References Committee, 2014, p 13). The committee was particularly concerned about the amount of time it took for schools to receive their results, thus reducing the diagnostic purpose of the process.

In 2014, Polesel and colleagues (2014) conducted the first national study of educators' views on the impact of NAPLAN. Over 8,000 educators from all states and territories participated. This study found that time spent on curriculum areas not assessed by the tests had reduced. Fifty-five per cent of teachers agreed or strongly agreed with the statement that 'NAPLAN narrows the range of teaching strategies that I use.' One commented: 'It puts pressure on teachers to change the emphasis from teaching for learning to teaching for test success' (cited in Polesel et al, 2014, p 648). As a result the authors concluded that 'Australian students' access to a wide and varied curriculum has been affected'. Other Australian studies into the effects of NAPLAN on teachers have produced similar findings (Comber, 2012; Klenowski and Wyatt-Smith, 2012; Thompson, 2013; Wyn et al, 2014).

Howell (2015, 2016) recorded the experiences of 105 children in two Queensland Catholic primary schools, through their drawings about NAPLAN and focus group discussions. Not all the children experienced NAPLAN as a negative event, but many noted a disjuncture between their everyday experiences of schooling, which included a diverse range of tasks supported by engaging in dialogue with their teachers and peers, and their experiences of test preparation, which included drills in how to complete the test, and needing to complete the task in isolation from their peers and teachers. NAPLAN was changing, and narrowing, their school experience.

These findings are probably not a surprise to educators working in English or Australian schools. In fact, our experience in teacher education tells us that many younger teachers are surprised that it was ever any different. These practices are the 'new normal' in England and becoming so in Australia. They reflect the experience of other countries too, particularly the United States (US) (Lipman, 2004; Nichols et al, 2006; Berliner, 2011; Ravitch, 2011) and New Zealand (Thrupp, 2018).

Holding students back

A common response to complaints that education is getting narrower and shallower is that it is regrettable but necessary. Although we might prefer students to be exposed to a broader range of subjects and experiences, a good grounding in maths and English is essential in modern knowledge economies. So, if time at schools becomes dominated by this kind of academic preparation, so be it. It is a price that needs to be paid for raising standards.

This argument, however, is not supported by the evidence. First, it is very far from being established that testing and target-setting regimes improve student achievement. Of course, the better prepared students are for tests, the better they will do in those tests. Every time a new set of tests is introduced, results on those tests improve year on year as teachers get more used to what is required and more skilled at getting children ready. But it is much less clear whether these gains in achievement are 'real' – in terms of greater knowledge or skills – or whether they are just the outcome of greater practice and focus on test items (Linn, 2001).

One indicator of this is international PISA tests, which are intended to show whether students can apply their understandings to real-life problems. As noted in Chapter 1, over the period in which national testing has been introduced into Australian schools, the performance of Australian teenagers in the PISA tests has steadily declined, while English PISA results have only shown significant improvement in one subject – maths (OECD, 2020b) – so it would not appear that excessive focusing on tests is helping with respect to what is tested in PISA. Importantly, PISA and NAPLAN test different kinds of outcomes, and it might be argued that raising literacy and numeracy standards results in less attention to standards intended to help students solve real-life problems.

At the top of the PISA league table there are countries and territories with intense testing regimes like Shanghai-China, but also those with very few standardised tests such as Finland (Tan and Reyes, 2018). More convincing, though, are detailed studies comparing students' work in different time periods. In the UK, Tymms (2004) studied the early period of primary school standard tests, analysing data from ten different sources of information about children's achievements and comparing these with the standard test data, which showed big increases in performance. He concluded that, in addition to grading procedures that meant the same grade was given to lower-quality work in later years, 'teaching to the test' accounted for much of the apparent rise.

Second, the practices associated with repeated tests may actually mean that students learn less, not more. To understand this, we need to turn to studies of educational practice, and the fundamental issue of how teachers teach. When teachers are preoccupied with getting through the material demanded in the test, the dominant means of knowledge transfer adopted in classrooms tends to be direct transmission from teachers to students through exposure and repetition of information. Students are rarely valued as active, informed participants in the learning process, or as co-producers of their own learning, and they are more likely to be seated in ability groups. These techniques reduce intellectual engagement. They may even put students off learning.

In the UK, maths education specialists Dr Maria Pampaka and Professor Julian Williams (2016) explored this quantitatively in a major study of the relationships between pedagogical approaches in mathematics, students' motivations and outcomes. They surveyed 132 teachers and around 13,000 of those teachers' students in Years 7 to 11, asking both groups about teaching practices, and grouping these into practices which were more 'transmissionist' (that is, they were about teachers conveying knowledge that the students needed for tests) and those that were more 'dialogic', 'connectionist' or 'interactive'. An unsurprising finding was that 'transmissionist' teaching increased during secondary school. But also, significantly, they found that when students perceived the teaching as 'transmissionist' there was a negative effect on students' mathematical dispositions – that is, their desire to engage with maths and study it in the future – even controlling for other factors. This effect was stronger for girls than boys. In Australia, a recent review of NAPLAN commissioned by the governments of NSW, Queensland,

Victoria and Australian Capital Territory raised concerns that an unintended effect of NAPLAN is the 'formulaic teaching of writing' and 'formulaic writing' being produced by students (McGaw et al, 2020, p 11). As in the study into mathematics in the UK, the review reported that the NAPLAN 'writing test is having a negative impact on children's and young people's enjoyment of writing, their creativity, and opportunities to express imagination in writing' (p 86).

Other studies of educational practice have elaborated on what goes missing from teaching and learning when teachers focus excessively on tests. In the late 2000s, Wyse and Torrance (2009) reviewed a large number of studies of primary education in England covering the period from the introduction of national curriculum tests. Among the key insights from their review were that pupils were less likely to help each other as a result of being seated in ability groups and a more competitive atmosphere; that teachers focused more on shorter answers rather than the development of more extended and complex writing; and that teachers became more directive, allowing children less time to explore and develop their own ideas. They concluded that the testing regime 'carries with it considerable risk to children's learning' (Wyse and Torrance, 2009, p 221). Jones (2010) found that time pressures related to testing, and the fact that national curriculum tests did not assess or always require higher-order thinking, meant that a focus on testing led to a reduction in the teaching of 'thinking skills' such as information processing, reasoning, enquiry and creative thinking as well as metacognition (often described as 'learning to learn'). As Kim (2011) has pointed out, opportunities for critical creative thinking are also lost when content such as the arts, sciences and enrichment programmes are squeezed out to make room for test preparation. Kim (2011) shows that in the US, there has been a steady and persistent decline in creative-thinking scores (as measured by the Torrance Tests of Creative Thinking) since 1990 among Americans of all ages, especially in kindergarten through to third grade, as testing regimes have become established and embedded.

So, it appears that rather than tests helping raise standards of achievement, they are creating dilemmas for teachers who need to trade off engaging their students in deep learning with preparing them to do well on tests.

Box 3.2: Test preparation and transmissionist teaching at Farrell High School

Following one of Ofsted's recommendations, the teacher-researchers at Farrell High School (Firth et al, 2014) set about identifying features of 'effective' pedagogies in their own subject department, with a view to sharing and growing these practices. Adopting a collective approach to teaching and observing each other's work against an agreed framework and set within a comprehensive and systematic approach to documenting, scrutinising and analysing their data, they identified a set of curricular-pedagogical features that were likely to have contributed towards students' engagement and performance. These included students' self-regulation and directing tasks in the lesson; questions being used to promote and develop student thinking; students engaging in activities requiring them to demonstrate intellectual quality; and students valuing what they were learning and its connectedness to the world beyond the classroom. Despite the efforts of teachers at Farrell to share and grow practices that reflected these types of quality teaching and learning, and the potential of these practices to positively influence student engagement, their adoption was displaced due to test preparation pressure. The performance of students on test results remained weak compared with similar schools on national data. Low test performance is often blamed on weak teaching practices. However, this example demonstrates that the implementation of such ('transmissionist') practices was due to the pressure on teachers to improve test performance. Teachers with the ability to implement quality learning experiences felt constrained to comply with test preparation. Consequently, students' learning outcomes were capped by the very curricular-pedagogical choices aimed at improving their test results.

Moreover, there are broader concerns about the effects of excessive testing on children's well-being. In Australia, the relatively recent introduction of testing regimes means that 'before' and 'after' effects can be discerned. For example, Wyn and colleagues (2014) studied 16 schools, of varying sizes, type and socioeconomic circumstances, in two Australian states. They found that students disliked NAPLAN and that the more tests they did, the more disinterested they became. It is particularly concerning that the majority of students consulted, across a range of contexts, reported feeling some stress associated with NAPLAN. 'A smaller number experienced anxiety and stress related conditions such as insomnia, physical reactions such as hyperventilation, profuse sweating, nail biting, headaches, stomach aches and migraines' (Wyn et al, 2014, p 6). Parents generally expressed more positive views towards NAPLAN than teachers, but about 40 per cent described signs of stress or anxiety exhibited by their children. These findings reflect the results of youth surveys in Australia that trace increasing concerns by young people over the past decade about 'coping with stress' and 'school and study problems' (Mission Australia, 2010; Bailey et al, 2016; Carlisle et al, 2019).

In England, the direct well-being effects of test regimes are hard to establish, since they have been established so long. There are some red flags, though. Children in England fare badly compared with those in other countries on liking school (Inchley et al, 2016; The Children's Society, 2018), self-efficacy, fear of failure and life satisfaction (OECD, 2020a), and relationships with teachers (Children's Worlds, 2016). The prevalence of anxiety and depressive disorders is increasing (Sadler et al, 2018). English 15-year-olds are relatively good at reading, but they read for pleasure much less than their peers in other countries (Sizmur et al, 2019). Not all the evidence is bad. For example, scores on liking school in England have improved slightly in recent years while test regimes have arguably tightened (The Children's Society, 2018). But the link to negative consequences is drawn by many people who work with children and young people. Beneath the survey findings are deep concerns about how the education system values and recognises young people and fosters their development. As one interviewee in Hutchings' (2015) study explained, 'some children never participate in learning that they actually enjoy and never experience any success' (2015, p 41), and teachers in special schools particularly highlighted how independence and life skills were sidelined and undervalued.

Importantly, holding children and young people back in this way is not just bad for them, it is bad for the economy, harming the higher-level skills and economic competitiveness that motivate the 'standards agenda' in the first place. In England, even the Confederation of British Industry has argued that 'the current exam system risks turning schools into exam factories that are churning out people who are not sufficiently prepared for life outside the school gates' and warns that 'a continuous treadmill of assessment' is failing to equip young people with the 'attitudes and behaviours' that are vital for success, including 'determination, optimism and emotional success' (Garner, 2014). Meanwhile in Australia, the Business Council of Australia (2018) has pointed out the need to 'future proof' the post-secondary education system by developing the kinds of skills and knowledge that will be crucial in producing more highly skilled flexible adaptable workers. An education dominated by tests looks problematic whatever one's view of what education is for.

Exacerbating inequalities

These findings tell us that a system dominated by testing can produce unintended negative effects for children across all schools and whatever their backgrounds. Here we are particularly concerned by what the evidence tells us about educational fairness, and the capacity of the system to help close early gaps in development and achievements caused by social and economic disadvantage, as well as cultural and racial differences.

One thing is very evident from many studies: the narrowing effect of tests on curriculum, and their tendency to restrict depth of learning, seems to be particularly prevalent in schools serving areas of high poverty and disadvantage. Where more learners are struggling to reach 'expected levels' in the tests, more effort has to be put into striving for these benchmarks above other valued outcomes from schooling. In Hutchings' (2015) study, most of the practices associated with pressure on schools to raise test scores, such as narrower curriculum and repeated test preparation, were more likely to occur in schools with high proportions of students from disadvantaged backgrounds. Within schools, these practices were more likely to affect children from disadvantaged backgrounds, as well as those with lower prior attainment and additional needs, because they were more likely to struggle to reach age-related expectations.

Hutchings (2015) pointed out that this also means children from disadvantaged backgrounds are more likely to continually experience 'failure' and more likely to become disaffected as they are repeatedly made to redo tests for which they are not developmentally ready. These findings are powerfully borne out in the testimonies of children and teachers by Professor Diane Reay in her book *Miseducation* (2017). Teachers explained how the dominance of testing made children detest education when it was about learning only how to pass tests, not about any life skills or enjoyment of learning. Primary school children expressed anxiety about their performance and explained how their failure to perform in tests would ruin their chances and consign them to lives of unemployment, low-skilled work, crime or hardship. In her research comparing Year 4 children in a 'working-class school' with a 'middle-class school', Hempel-Jorgensen (2009) found that children had different identities as learners and concepts of 'the ideal pupil'. Those in the working-class school, where pedagogy was dominated by test preparation, adopted ideals of compliance and discipline. Those in the middle-class school believed teachers liked them to be clever and funny.

The impact of extra help on low-achieving students is echoed in the findings of Hutchings' (2015) study, which noted that lower-attaining pupils (including those as young as six) are removed from other lessons to do extra maths and English, and 'miss out on the art and the PE [physical education] and the history and the geography and the ICT [information and communications technology]' (p 41). As one teacher in Hutchings' study put it, '[t]heir experience at school must be horrible – in assembly they've got to do phonics intervention, then a phonics lesson, a literacy lesson, a maths lesson, lunch, reading, extra reading intervention and then speech intervention. What else are they learning about the world?' (cited in Hutchings, 2015, p 41).

According to University of Hull academics Dr Lisa Jones and Dr Josef Ploner, these more limited experiences apply not just to the regular curriculum, but to wider opportunities. Their study of the involvement of schools in Hull with the year-long UK City of Culture (CoC) initiative in 2017 showed that the extent

Box 3.3: The particular effects of testing practices in low SES schools

In the case of **six Queensland primary schools** there is evidence of considerable time spent on test preparation across school types. Ian Hardy (2015) described significant pressure to ensure improved student outcomes on tests, and a prevailing logic of active test preparation that justified the allotment of considerable time in the form of meetings strategising for NAPLAN, and 'hours of preparation specifically for the test' each week (2015, p 351). Additional staffing resources were routinely diverted to test preparation. A narrow curriculum was further narrowed for students who performed poorly on NAPLAN and received additional help in core subjects in lieu of participation in regular timetabled classes in other parts of the curriculum. In schools in low SES settings, the test preparation included a considerable amount of time practising tests and assisting students to learn words likely to be included, such as NAPLAN-style dictation, entering missing words, circling misspelt words, and 'colouring in "bubbles" beside multiple choice answers' (p 351). Students were also constantly tested to determine whether they should continue to receive intensive, ongoing interventions. A consequence was that students in low SES settings were exposed to an 'adumbrated' curriculum that denied them the opportunity to engage in broad and stimulating knowledge that might assist them to develop ideas that could enrich their writing, reading and numeracy practices (p 357).

to which schools could engage with CoC was severely affected by the socioeconomic context of the schools. Successful schools in middle-class areas welcomed it and found room to engage, but these opportunities could not be extended to working-class children in schools with lower attainment because of the intense pressure to focus on raising attainment in core curriculum subjects (Jones and Ploner, 2019).

So while extensive focus on testing may be motivated by an egalitarian desire to make sure that everyone is able to acquire the knowledge and skills they need to do well in life, the reality seems to be that the least advantaged children end up being subjected to school and classroom experiences that are narrower and less enriching, and that put them off education and make them feel like failures. These circumstances are more likely to exacerbate inequalities than to remedy them.

4

Schooling that works for some but not for others

One thing about which there seems to be near universal consensus among education policy makers is that education systems should provide equally for all children and provide the opportunity of success for all.

This holds whether you start from the position of the United Nations (UN) goal to 'Ensure inclusive and equitable quality education and promote lifelong learning opportunities for all' (United Nations, 2015) or from the UN Convention on the Rights of the Child, Article 29, which states that 'Education must develop every child's personality, talents and abilities to the full' (UNICEF, 1992). It holds if you start from goals to reduce inequalities, enhance social mobility and foster social justice, or if you start from economic aspirations to increase human capital, maximise productivity and spend less on welfare. Inclusive and equitable education is, in theory, a 'no-brainer'.

But it isn't happening. In fact, in far too many cases, children and young people who need the education system most are actually getting *less* from it than their more advantaged peers. That uncomfortable fact has long been recognised, at least by sociologists of education if not always by politicians. But there is also evidence that the system is *increasingly* marginalising children who in different ways rely on it most. Instead of compensating for other injustices, the education system may increasingly be making them worse.

Unequal access to schooling

One major factor in the production of educational divisions is the structure of school systems, including differences between and within sectors that make up these systems. This may seem too obvious even to state. Yet it is striking how reluctant policy makers are to recognise these differences. Instead, they put a lot of emphasis and effort into what individual teachers and leaders can do rather than taking action to level up young people's access to schooling resources. So, it is worth restating these long-term features of schooling before moving on to more recent developments.

In England, the 'elephant in the room' in discussions of education policy and inequalities is the private school system: small, politically hard-to-touch and incredibly influential in the production of the elite (The Sutton Trust and the Social Mobility Commission, 2019). A recent review of inequalities from University College London and the economic think tank the Resolution Foundation reported that not only is the progress made by privately educated children significantly greater at every education stage than for state-educated children, but that those educated privately also get better returns to the same qualifications because of the investment such schools make in extra-curricular activities, cultural activities and soft skills development (Morris et al, 2019).

Other structural differences produce distinctions between schools. In England there are well-established hierarchies of schools, with academically selective schools (grammars) and elite comprehensive schools at the top that attract more socially advantaged students. Similar hierarchies exist in Australia and are driven by deliberate policies to enhance parental choice through growth in low fee-paying independent schools, such that the national government is now a minority public funder of the state-administered government sector and the majority public funder for non-government schools. Government schools with selective intakes and high concentrations of middle-class children remain popular with parents who have the capacity to make schooling choices.

Top schools in England and Australia are better resourced through fundraising from parents (Brown, 2020; Rowe and Perry, 2020b). They are often better connected, through parents and alumni, to wealthy individuals, firms or charities who can provide visits, work experience, or careers advice. Capacity to attract and retain good teachers varies a lot in England, even though schools may have equal funding. As a recent commission on inequality in education led by former Liberal Democrat leader Nick Clegg found, schools in poorer areas are much more likely to have teachers without relevant subject degrees and their staff are much more likely to leave than those in richer areas, resulting in fewer experienced and well-qualified staff where they are needed most (Clegg et al, 2017).

So it is not surprising that schools in the poorest areas that are the hardest to staff are judged to be of lower quality than those in affluent neighbourhoods. In England in 2019, over 90 per cent of secondary schools in the least deprived fifth of neighbourhoods were adjudged outstanding or good, compared with 64 per cent in the most deprived, and with a steady social gradient in between (Ofsted, 2019b). There are particular difficulties in peripheral areas: isolated coastal areas in the south of England together with areas in the north and Midlands were identified in Ofsted's 2014/15 annual report as representing 'a divided nation' because children in these areas 'are much less likely to attend a good or outstanding secondary school than those in the rest of the country' (Ofsted, 2015, p 9).

The Staff in Australia's Schools Surveys show that schools in rural and remote areas experience more difficulty attracting and retaining suitable staff than those in provincial and metropolitan areas (McKenzie et al, 2014). Principals who experience staff shortages report using a range of coping strategies including recruiting less qualified teachers, requiring teachers to teach outside their field of expertise, combining classes across year levels, or recruiting teachers on short-term contracts (McKenzie et al, 2014, p 129).

So, although it is nothing new, it remains the case that the structure of our education systems enables better-off people to access more and better educational opportunities. Rather than the most disadvantaged pupils getting access to the better resources and higher-quality schools, the situation is generally the other way round.

> ## Box 4.1: Coastal academy secondary schools: school leaders getting a fair deal for students
>
> A recurring theme in interviews conducted with the leaders in the case of six coastal academy secondary schools was 'getting a fair deal' for their students (Passy and Ovenden-Hope, 2020, p 229) in contexts with limited resources and limited possibility for future qualifications. These leaders deployed strategies to provide enriching experiences that might support young people to become active decision makers and to 'understand the nature of the choices they were making about their future' (p 11). Turning their schools around so that students were passing examinations was a high priority but not their only one. Pragmatically, they acknowledged the need to work 'with the grain of the system while not necessarily agreeing with it' (p 9). They shared a commitment to affording their students opportunities to develop new skills and understandings, and engage in new and challenging experiences in addition to those required to improve test performance. They hoped that by providing a wide range of educational experiences, young people might be able to play a more active role in shaping their own futures and overcoming the structural inequities they experienced due to their social and spatial location, 'allowing them to grow in terms of confidence in their entitlement to education and their ability to participate' (p 10). The leaders of these coastal academies maintained a belief in the capacity of education to be an emancipatory influence in the lives of young people who, through no fault of their own, were missing out on resources and opportunities available to their peers in other places.

Unequal school experiences

Within schools too, students from different backgrounds and with different characteristics can have very different experiences. One issue is simply the cost of the school day: the additional fees and charges that can inadvertently exclude students whose families have very little spare income from the opportunities that others enjoy for extra-curricular enrichment experiences (Treanor, 2018; Rowe and Perry, 2020a). Large inequalities exist between government schools in Australia due to the greater capacity of schools in more affluent areas to collect 'voluntary fees'. These schools receive more than four times the parent financial contributions than schools in areas where parents have less capacity to contribute, and these contributions can be put towards enhanced learning resources that are not generally available in other government schools (Rowe and Perry, 2020a). Young people are aware of the potential burden on families with limited resources of schooling costs, and they report choosing a secondary school based on their understanding of the associated costs (Skattebol et al, 2012, p 118).

Practices of ability grouping also play a major part in stratifying school experiences. Ability grouping is the norm in England (Dracup, 2014), despite abundant research evidence showing that it has no significant benefits for attainment overall, and negative effects on students in lower sets (Boaler and Wiliam, 2001; Hallam et al, 2003; Hallam and Parsons, 2013; Education Endowment Foundation, 2015). In Australia, ability grouping is not uncommon, but it is hard to quantify its prevalence. However, teachers report that performative agendas and policies have encouraged these practices to flourish (Spina, 2019).

Ability grouping perpetuates inequalities because students with fewer advantages outside school are more likely to be placed in lower sets and streams (Francis et al, 2017a). This means that, in addition to any effects of the school or area they are in, they are more likely than other students in their school to be assigned less experienced and lower-status teachers (Allen and Sims, 2018). They may also get access to a more limited curriculum that offers fewer opportunities. Australian evidence has shown how students from low socioeconomic groups are more likely to be assigned to low-status curriculum subjects (Teese, 2000), and receive low-quality, low-level, low-weight vocational training (Polesel, 2008) as subject selection and timetables act as a kind of 'cognitive architecture' to shape different curricular pathways (Teese and Polesel, 2003).

In England, when a wide range of vocational qualifications were included as equivalent qualifications to GCSEs in school performance tables, some schools effectively operated two 'tracks', with the less academic students losing access to subjects like history, languages and music and focusing almost entirely on English, maths and vocational subjects (Wrigley, 2014). And these divisions by 'ability' turn into self-fulfilling prophecies, as Francis and colleagues found in their major study of over 11,000 English 11- and 12-year-olds. Set placement was correlated with self-confidence in the set subject and also with general self-confidence in learning, as pupils internalised these judgements of their 'ability' (Francis et al, 2017b).

All this matters regardless of whether students are in the 'right' stream or set according to their prior attainment. Making matters worse, research studies show how certain groups of students are persistently misallocated to lower groups because teachers use other factors such as group size, behaviour, relationship management and parental pressure to determine group allocation and because their judgements may be clouded by stereotypical assumptions. Most affected are children from lower SES families, minority ethnic groups (Black and Asian children in England; First Nations, Pacifika and some groups of migrant children in Australia) and girls (for maths), although boys are also misallocated, often on behavioural grounds (Muijs and Dunne, 2010; Macqueen, 2013; Connolly et al, 2019).

And students do not just have unequal experiences of school because of affordability issues and grouping practices. They also experience the curriculum differently when curriculum materials fail to represent their lives and experiences. In England, this long-standing issue has recently resurfaced prominently with the return to a more 'traditional' curriculum since 2010. Teachers in Neumann and colleagues' (2020) study described how the new curriculum was inappropriate in their multi-ethnic classrooms because it had 'squashed a sense of diversity, because we do fewer women writers ... fewer writers of colour', and the GCSE English curriculum had become 'monocultural', with 'really dry, nineteenth century texts, non-literary, non-fiction, and fiction, just a sort of obsession with the nineteenth century' (Neumann et al, 2020, p 708). And Wrigley (2018) uses an example from the 2016 KS2 reading test to illustrate how the choice of materials can work to the advantage of some students:

> Maria and Oliver are attending a party in the garden of a house that used to belong to Maria's family.

> They sneak away to explore the grounds. Maria and Oliver were quite a distance from the party when they found the little rowing boat in the grassy shallows of a small lake beyond the garden. Glancing nervously behind her, Maria suggested that they row out to the island in the middle of the lake. Oliver looked at her questioningly. Maria explained that there was a secret monument on the island to one of her ancestors. (Wrigley, 2018, p 273)

As Wrigley explains, this apparently neutral test of comprehension might be totally incomprehensible to children who have never come across families with ancestral homes or grounds or parties that involve rowing on private lakes, disadvantaging them in the test. More broadly, persistent representation only of the lives of more privileged students is likely to make others feel marginalised and unrecognised – a form of symbolic power at work.

Schooling practices can lead young people to pick up very different messages about their value as learners and people who are linked to their cultural background. In Australia, this is particularly the case for Aboriginal and Torres Strait Islander children. In terms of their underachievement on performance measures (Thomson et al, 2019), studies have shown that the problem to be addressed is not the First Nations status of students, but the implicit negative stereotypes held by teachers (Moodie et al, 2019). The pervasiveness of these beliefs extends to these students, who also perceive themselves as low achieving. Internalised racism not only weakens their belief in their ability to achieve similar results to other young people, it also contributes to disengagement, emotional distress and school withdrawal (Moodie et al, 2019, p 289).

Race is also a factor in English schools. For example, Black boys at Dreamfields were more likely to be shouted at for talking than their White British or Asian peers (Kulz, 2017, p 139). Children from poorer homes were also more likely to be shouted at, and to enjoy school less, according to Horgan's (2007) study of the impact of poverty on young people's experiences of school. Children and young people interviewed by Reay (2017) and Bright (2011) described teachers looking down on them and dismissing their aspirations. Smith and Todd's (2016) evaluation of a programme of 'poverty proofing' described young children's feelings of disconnection, stigma and shame when teachers seemed to assume shared experiences that are actually out of range for poorer households.

Box 4.2: City Campus: keeping kids engaged and improving their life chances

Diagnosed at an early age with a major sight impediment, Liam had not received medical help for his condition, and his family experienced extreme social and economic isolation. After attending multiple schools, Liam's assessment of City Campus as 'the greatest school I've ever been to' invites reflection on what he had to say about his previous experiences, and what is was about City Campus that enabled him to engage with and continue his education (McInerney and Smyth, 2014, p 245). He reported frequent experiences of bullying in previous schools but none at City Campus. Teachers modified their practices to accommodate his disability and support him to persist with learning and pursue his big interest in music. He was assigned an aide to sit alongside him in class. Unlike the music teacher at one school who 'was no good ... and just gave [him] theory notes he couldn't read', Liam stated that the music teachers at City Campus have 'taught [him] heaps ... Teachers aren't afraid to jump in and have fun here' (p 245). Although he failed two subjects the previous year, he was taking 'the academic route' to higher education (p 246) with a combination of academic and vocational subjects. In his story of schooling Liam identifies the personal challenges he faced that in prior settings presented barriers to staying engaged in education and were likely to have contributed to him being 'consigned to an at-risk category of disengaged learners, underachievers and potential school dropouts' (p 244). At City Campus, Liam was supported in myriad ways – including through radically different relations between teachers and students – to successfully complete Year 12. The opportunity to combine vocational and academic subjects contributed to his enjoyment of school. Liam's life circumstances lacked many opportunities, but he fortuitously found his way to a school that improved his life chances. His story reinforces the need for such opportunities to be hardwired into schooling systems, and not left to chance.

We do not wish to claim that nothing has changed in the interests of making schools more inclusive places. When a young person's desire to learn is met with productive activities and supportive resources responsive to the realities of their lives, Skattebol and colleagues (2012) have observed that they are able to 'map out routes towards secure economic futures'. Problems arise when their aspirations, and those of their families, are not well supported but 'have a shaky futures orientation – an orientation that [does] not always translate into engagement' (Skattebol et al, 2012, p 115).

Along with the effects of tests reported in Chapter 3, these examples suggest other reasons why children from groups in society who experience a high level of poverty and other forms of social exclusion and marginalisation in both England and Australia say that they do not feel they belong in school. According to the OECD's PISA programme, in Australia the rate of school belonging fell from 88% in 2003 to 68% in 2018, and in the UK (figures for England not given) from 85% to 62% in the same period (OECD, 2004, 2020a). As the OECD explains, school belonging matters because 'it is only when students are physically present, and are mentally ready to learn, that they can make the most of the opportunities schools provide' (OECD, 2017, p 30). If the least advantaged students do not feel they belong in school, educational inequalities will widen.

Not in school

Lastly, we come to the problem of children and young people who are excluded from the system altogether. Exclusions from school are currently increasing and, most worryingly, there is increasing evidence that this is happening because it is in the interests of schools, not in the interests of students for whom different provision might work better.

In England, there are two types of exclusion from a school: permanent and fixed-period exclusion. In Australia, exclusion and suspension are the more common terms, respectively, but enrolment cancellation and fixed-term exclusion are also used. In England, both types of exclusion had been on the decrease for a ten-year period up to 2013/14. However, since then the numbers have been increasing to the extent that the House of Commons Education Committee (2018) described it as a 'scandal'. In state-funded secondary schools, the rate of fixed-period exclusion rose from 6.6 per cent of the school population in 2010–14 to 10.1 per cent in 2017–18, and permanent exclusions from 0.06 per cent of the school population to 0.1 per cent in the same period. In Australia, there is no national database to track school exclusion, and states have different policies. However, research conducted by Linda Graham (2018) in the state of Queensland reports that for the 12-year period 2006–17 inclusive, enrolment cancellations increased by 320 per cent and suspensions increased by 110 per cent.

The most obvious reason for rising exclusions is that behaviour in schools is getting worse. In England there is some evidence for this. In its annual survey of teachers, which attracts over 5,000 responses, one of the largest teacher unions – the National Association of Schoolmasters Union of Women Teachers (NASUWT) – shows that over the same period that exclusions have been rising, growing numbers of teachers have reported that they think there is a widespread behaviour problem in their schools – from 37 per cent in 2014 to 56 per cent in 2019 (NASUWT, 2019). But education reforms and policies can also contribute. Graham (2018) attributed a rapid spike in the rate of cancellations in 2014 to the extension of principals' disciplinary power giving them greater autonomy and power to suspend, including the ability to suspend for matters unrelated to the school. In Australia, McGregor and colleagues (2017) have highlighted that actual exclusions may be higher than those recorded because young people are asked or pressured to leave, and they experience feeling 'kicked out' (p 55) – a consequence of negative relations with teachers and peers, punitive discipline, a lack of learning support, and non-meaningful curricula.

According to England's House of Commons Education Committee (2018, p 14), it is the government's 'strong focus on school standards' that has 'led to school environments and practices that have resulted in disadvantaged children being disproportionately excluded'. They criticised zero-tolerance behaviour policies that could lead to some young people spending much of their time at school in 'isolation units' (solitary confinement) or being excluded for single misdemeanours, as well as 'off-rolling' – the practice of excluding students whose predicted academic performance in external examinations would not make a positive contribution to the school's league table performance. Increasing numbers of 'managed moves' and 'off-rollments' have also recently been reported by the Education Datalab (Nye, 2017) and Ofsted (Ofsted, 2019a; Rowe et al, 2019). The House of Commons Education Committee argued that some schools were showing a 'lack of moral accountability' (2018, p 14). It recommended that government should remind all schools of their responsibilities to children under the UN Convention on the Rights of the Child, which as well as committing educators to the development of all children's personalities, talents and abilities, states that 'discipline in schools must respect children's dignity and their rights' (House of Commons Education Committee, 2018, p 11).

In yet another damming report, England's Children's Commissioner, Anne Longfield, found that the number of children being educated at home had doubled in five years, mainly because their needs were not being met at school. For thousands of children, 'there is no school where they fit in' in 'an unforgiving school system which appears to have lost the kindness, the skill or the patience to keep them' (Children's Commissioner, 2019, p 2). Longfield cited harsh and inflexible behaviour policies and cuts to support staff as key issues, and asked, 'When did schools become like this?' (Children's Commissioner, 2019, p 2). She also reported the extensive use of isolation units or isolation 'booths' – 'spaces in which pupils sit in silence for hours as punishment for breaking school rules and disruptive behaviour' (Weale, 2020). In one case this was a 'portable booth made of cardboard used to place over a child in the classroom' (Weale, 2020). These practices are common enough to have been the focus of a conference held in early 2020 in England called 'Lose the Booths'.

Crucially, a consistent finding of research into school exclusion, whether formal or 'voluntary', is that it does not happen equally. The practice has the greatest impact on children who already experience forms of social exclusion, including those in out-of-home care, children with SEN and disabilities, children living in poverty and those from particular ethnic groups. In England, in the 2017–18 school year, pupils with SEN were six times as likely to be excluded than pupils without these needs; pupils eligible for FSM four times; and Black Caribbean pupils nearly three times as likely as the school population as a whole. Twenty-two per cent of children withdrawn from school to be home-educated also had SEN. In the absence of national figures for Australia, the report of the NSW Ombudsman (2017) provides comparative data about suspension and exclusion rates in NSW. In 2015, while Aboriginal students comprised 7 per cent of full-time equivalent (FTE) enrolments in NSW public schools, they comprised 24 per cent of short suspensions, and 27 per cent of long suspensions (NSW Ombudsman, 2017 p 39). Exclusions are also concentrated in particular schools, especially regional and remote areas (NSW Ombudsman, 2017). This is not just because children are dealing with more complex challenges that affect their conduct at school, but because schools are under greater pressure to increase their rates of academic achievement or to demonstrate good behaviour to parents and school inspectors. The incentives for them to exclude young people with complex and challenging behaviour are greater.

Exclusion from school might not be such a big worry if the young people excluded were able to make a fresh start in equally good provision. This is of course the objective. In England, local authorities have a duty to arrange alternative provision (AP) which can be in PRUs run by a local authority or in an AP academy or free school. In Australia, students who disengage from mainstream schools, which include settings where students are removed for intensive behavioural and educational support, may have the option of attending alternative education programmes, but demand outstrips supply. Consequently, some young people who are most in need of educational services are unable to access them (Mills and McGregor, 2016a).

AP is not all bad by any means, but it is patchy, and some areas have no good provision since teachers are less qualified and there are more supply teachers, leadership vacancies, and difficulties releasing staff to continuing professional development (CPD). The small size of schools often means a narrower curriculum (Plows et al, 2016; House of Commons Education Committee, 2018). Outcomes for young people who end up in AP tend to be very much weaker than for other young people – a result both of their previous disadvantages and the limitations of the provision. In England, just 4.5 per cent of children who attended AP achieved good passes in English and mathematics at GCSE, compared with 65.1 per cent in state-funded mainstream schools. They were seven times as likely not to carry on in education, employment or training after leaving school and were disproportionately represented in the criminal justice system. For some young people who rely on alternative provision, Mills and McGregor remind us that simply attending school should be considered an achievement due to the trauma they have experienced: 'The choice for these young people is often not between attending an alternative school or a mainstream school, but a choice between an alternative school or no school' (2016a, p 79).

Thus, despite the intentions of policy makers to create equitable systems that develop everyone's talents and abilities, the reality is that the young people who rely most on schooling to secure their educational pathways and contribute to their long-term well-being are least likely to be in well-resourced and effective schools in the first place, least likely to get the full benefit of the curricular and extra-curricular resources in their schools, and more likely to be marginalised within them or excluded from them, thus ending up in weaker provision still. Some of these problems are very long-standing, and some of them have recently been getting worse. They are hard to tackle but cannot be avoided if we want our education systems to be better and fairer.

5

Teachers making less of a difference

Many teachers say they joined the profession to make a difference, perhaps because they themselves experienced the transformative influence of a good teacher or tried their hand at a less fulfilling occupation. Whatever the reason, making a difference in the lives of young people is widely valued as a reason for joining and staying in a challenging profession. Take, for example, Belinda Lyons-Lee (2019), who took a year off teaching and became a published author. Despite the fewer demands and less pressure of her writing career, she returned to teaching because 'I needed to reconnect with my passion of introducing these teenagers to the power of a narrative to change a life and then introduce them to the skills so they could write their own powerful narrative that would change lives' (Lyons-Lee, 2019).

One of the most important functions of schooling is to help each young person to develop the narrative of their life, even when there are interruptions and when they face barriers beyond their control. Teachers' work fundamentally affects young people's experiences of schooling, but more than this it affects the likelihood that they will enjoy and succeed not only at school, but also in life.

In this chapter, we argue that in England and Australia, teachers are making less of a difference than they could, because of the ways in which their work is changing. Instead of concentrating their efforts on teaching, and on reviewing and developing their pedagogical practice, they are burdened by administrative demands associated with monitoring and demonstrating the performance of their students. These activities are described by a teacher in Comber and Nixon's (2009) study as 'meaningless bullshit destined for a cupboard in someone's office' (p 339). Within the classroom too, their teaching is increasingly prescribed, following a script or formula. In Chapter 3, we showed how 'teaching to the test' is making for a narrowing of learning opportunities for students. Here we unpack that further. Drawing on large-scale surveys of teachers conducted in England, Australia and across the globe, as well as in-depth studies of schools and classrooms, we relate teachers' widespread concerns with forced over-compliance, superficial regulations and the erosion of professional autonomy. We show how the practices associated with increasing accountability are constraining teachers' pedagogical repertoires and skills, diminishing trust in the teaching profession and, ultimately, making teaching and school leadership a job that fewer people want to do.

Too much focus on activities that fail to improve teaching and learning

For some years, close-up studies of teachers' work have been pointing to increasing demands on their time for non-teaching tasks, often related to school accountability and to centrally driven policy reforms. In England, studies from the 1990s onwards – after the Education Reform Act 1988 (see Chapter 6) – have reported a steady erosion of teachers' long-standing autonomy over learning and the curriculum in favour of more 'technician-type' roles, 'delivering' predefined subject content and learning outcomes, and demonstrating their compliance and effectiveness (Dadds, 1997; Ball, 2003b; Stevenson, 2007). In Australia, even prior to the introduction of NAPLAN, teachers reported increasing 'bureaucratic' requirements related to demands of 'reform' and 'quality' (Comber and Nixon, 2009) or, put another way, surveillance and policing that resulted in their having to complete and lodge endless forms and records (Carlson, 2005). In Comber and Nixon's study, teachers also noted the impact of 'constant change' in curriculum documents and policy guidelines with a push to 'line up our curriculum with frameworks and make that visible' (2009, p 339). More of their time was taken up with tasks that did not have a clear sense of purpose or worthwhile outcome.

However, over the past five years, evidence that teachers' work is being distorted in ways that take them away from core teaching and learning activities has been coming thick and fast as large-scale surveys of teachers have become increasingly common. Every five years, since 2008, the OECD has asked teachers and school leaders about their working conditions, learning environments and practices. In 2018, the Teaching and Learning International Survey (TALIS) (OECD, 2019) of lower secondary-level teachers (teaching students aged 11– 14) included around 2,400 teachers in England and around 3,600 in Australia. The results confirmed previous results that teachers in both countries are generally working longer hours and doing more administration and marking than most of their counterparts internationally. Teachers in England were working approximately 47 hours per week, and those in Australia 45 hours a week compared with an average of around 39 hours across OECD countries (that is, 20 per cent and 15 per cent more respectively). In both cases, this was not because they were teaching longer hours but because they were spending more time, compared with teachers in other countries, on marking and general administration. For example, English teachers reported spending 6.2 hours on marking compared with the average of 4.2, and Australian teachers reported spending 4.1 hours on general administration compared with the average of 2.7. In England, 65 per cent of lower secondary teachers thought they spent too much time on marking, and 72 per cent thought they spent too much time on administration (Jerrim and Sims, 2019). In Australia, 24 per cent of teachers reported experiencing stress in their work 'a lot', which is higher than the OECD average (18 per cent). Administrative tasks and having too much marking were two of the main causes of stress (OECD, 2018).

The TALIS results confirmed evidence from national and sub-national surveys. For instance, in Australia, a study of more than 18,000 teachers in the state of NSW concluded 'that vastly increased administrative tasks are having a "blanketing" effect across all types of schools, locations, levels of socioeconomic advantage and staff teaching roles within schools, and severely threaten to overwhelm teachers' professional focus on teaching and student learning' (McGrath-Champ et al, 2018, p 5). Similarly, in 2014, 43,832 teachers in England responded to an online consultation about their workloads, including a question about 'unnecessary and unproductive tasks which take up too much of your time'. Over half of the participants cited 'excessive/depth of marking – detail and frequency required' and 'recording, inputting, monitoring and analysing data' as tasks that were excessive and burdensome (Gibson et al, 2015).

In England, these findings were so striking and so concerning that the government, to its credit, established three independent teacher workload review groups, made up largely of school leaders and teachers, to gather more evidence and advise on what should be done. Their findings got to the nub of the problems. It was not marking or administration per se that teachers were complaining about – assessment is an important element of pedagogical practice, and teachers' work already involves numerous such tasks, such as attendance, curriculum mapping, and so on. Rather, it was the piling on of meaningless tasks that took enormous amounts of teachers' time without corresponding benefits to students.

One of these was a practice known as 'deep marking' (sometimes known as 'triple marking') in which teachers provide written feedback to pupils, pupils then respond in writing and this is then checked and verified by the teacher to demonstrate that feedback has been given and received. Or, as one primary school teacher in the consultation put it: 'Marking every last shred of work with developmental and next step marking, checking that the children have responded to the marking and getting them to respond to yesterday's marking as well as today's marking, and marking that they have read my marking and so on ad infinitum' (middle leader, primary school in England, cited in Independent Teacher Workload Review Group, 2016a, p 6).

According to the review group on marking and to a review of the evidence commissioned by DfE (Elliott et al, 2016), there is no evidence at all of any benefits of deep marking or indeed of some of the other excessive marking practices that were being complained about. And that probably is no surprise to many teachers. A frequent concern raised in the consultation was that much of the marking is not actually done for the benefit of the children/students in the first place, but for the benefit of senior leadership teams to reassure them (and Ofsted) that everything is being done that could be done to maximise attainment. In some schools, teachers even reported having to mark (with the notation 'VF') aspects of students' work on which they had given verbal feedback. Too often, the review group said, 'it is the marking itself which is being monitored and commented on by leaders rather than pupil outcomes and progress as a result of quality feedback' (Independent Teacher Workload Review Group, 2016a, p 6).

Similar problems were reported in relation to lesson planning. Exceptionally detailed plans, including annotated seating plans for each lesson and having to change and revisit plans during the course of the week, were expected – not because these practices were more beneficial to students, but to provide 'false comfort' to school management (Independent Teacher Workload Review Group, 2016b). Teachers reported spending evenings and weekends producing detailed plans that went into folders for the school to give to Ofsted inspectors. The review group on this issue stated that detailed planning had become a 'box-ticking' exercise that was unhelpful and burdensome. Similarly, the review group on data found that it is 'often used too much for monitoring and compliance, rather than to support pupil learning and school improvement' (Teacher Workload Advisory Group, 2018, p 4). While data collection and analysis are smaller parts of a teachers' job than marking and planning, teachers are most likely to cite them as a waste of time because it is not clear what they are for.

The 2018 TALIS survey mentioned earlier showed that, compared with the 2013 survey, English secondary head teachers were spending an extra ten hours a week on leadership and administration tasks, with correspondingly less time on curriculum and teaching-related tasks, student interactions and interactions with communities and businesses. Studies of leaders in Australia show that they also complain of too much time focusing not on teaching and learning but on matters like managing school image/external relations, preparing for inspection, reporting to parents and to authorities (compliance) and negotiating their school's survival (Cranston, 2013; McGrath-Champ et al, 2019). In Australia's largest state, NSW, a study of principal workload and time use conducted by Deloitte (2017) for the NSW Department of Education found that principals as a group feel overwhelmed by their workload: 75 per cent of respondents reported that their workload was not achievable, and 77 per cent reported that it was not sustainable. There was no significant difference by school type, location, size or socioeconomic status of children's families in the distribution of time spent across activities undertaken by school leaders.

While one of our primary concerns is that education policies frequently hit harder in schools that cater for the children of families experiencing high levels of poverty and difference, the findings in this chapter suggest that increased administrative workloads are experienced across all types of schools. Although there does not appear to be strong evidence of a socioeconomic gradient in the distribution of these practices, the question that needs to be asked is whether intensifying the administrative demands on teachers and leaders pays off and improves the educational experiences and outcomes of students. The evidence here needs to be closely examined to identify the educational benefits that are likely to be derived from the intensification of administrative tasks.

The adoption of whole-school administrative and pedagogical approaches are a means by which the resources of a school can be focused on the achievement of a collective set of outcomes, but it requires school leaders and teachers to be conscripted for this purpose. Consequently, they are required to forgo some degrees of freedom when exercising their professional judgement because the range of pedagogical and leadership practices that might otherwise be available are subsumed by collective agreements and monitored by surveillance techniques intended to ensure compliance. The example of Parkside demonstrates that this can be successful in improving student achievement and it is a welcome intervention by at least some teachers, but a consequence is that both teaching and learning are more reductive and scripted. Again, this has the potential to focus the attention of teachers and leaders on agreed outcomes but

---

Box 5.1: Parkside Academy: the controlling effects of school autonomy on teachers' work

In England, the formation of academies promised relief from the administrative burden of bureaucratic and inefficient public governance, and the potential for more agile and flexible autonomous forms of management to drive improvement through collaboration, innovation and experimentation. Parkside is part of a multi-academy trust. In the early years of Parkside, administrative autonomy afforded school leaders the opportunity to turn what was considered to be 'a challenging and potentially dangerous environment into a context that became safe and supportive of learning' (Salokangas and Ainscow, 2018, p 51). Order was imposed through the consistent adoption of standardised, school-wide approaches to classroom layout, homework, bookwork, lesson planning and Ofsted-style inspections of teachers each term. These processes shaped the work of department heads and assistant principals towards compliance monitoring. Some teachers experienced the reduction of pedagogical choices as supportive, while others found it constraining, but all were subject to high levels of control and pressure to adopt the chosen administrative routines and one-size-fits-all approaches to teaching. Despite the increased autonomy available to local leaders at Parkside, teachers were 'subject to similar, if not greater, control as their colleagues in other types of publicly funded schools' (p 127). Progress was made in the early years of Parkside as reflected in improved performance in public examinations by students, many of whom were from poorer backgrounds, but it came at a cost to students' educational experiences, which became more narrowly focused around test performance.

---

it should be acknowledged that it underutilises and constrains the professional skills and judgements of teachers, and requires their compliance with practices that they may not agree with or value, as illustrated in the following examples drawn from our case study schools.

- At Dreamfields, students remain silent in class and as they move between classes. This practice is achieved through the continual collective action of teachers, including the use of the 'verbal cane' (Kulz, 2017, p 75) to shout at students to reinforce order and expectations. It is a form of discipline that some teachers took issue with and believed was inappropriate.
- At Parkside, teachers were expected to use a 'traffic lights' system, in which students indicated their level of

understanding by holding up red-, amber- or green-coloured cards (Salokangas and Ainscow, 2018). Some teachers did not trust or value the system, which relied on students declaring their lack of understanding by holding up a red card. Yet, not adopting this approach had consequences, such as failing an inspection by school leaders.

- At the Northern primary schools, highly experienced teachers were expected to adopt explicit teaching approaches, such as requiring students to display their knowledge and practice of spelling through the correct placement of capital letters and full stops, and words that were positioned a finger space apart (Hayes et al, 2017). The substantive purpose of communicating something meaningful was stripped away, and teachers who were otherwise committed to high-quality outcomes managed students and kept them busy by implementing the practices that were asked of them.

Problems with teacher recruitment and retention

Teachers making less of a difference than they could is a matter of concern, especially in communities that most need high-quality teachers, because it removes one of the key reasons why teachers accept the difficulties and challenges of working in these contexts – the opportunity to make a difference. Weakening this incentive causes a broader problem too. It makes teaching a less attractive and satisfying job and depletes the profession of experienced educators and talented new recruits.

In England, there are problems both with recruitment and retention of teachers. The number of people enrolling on initial teacher training courses has been below target for the past seven years. At the same time, the number of teachers leaving the profession after training is rising. Around one fifth of teachers leave within the first two years of teaching and one third within the first five years, a worrying statistic when research shows that teachers, on average, reach a peak of effectiveness after between five and eight years and are then able to sustain that high level for a decade or more (Ellis et al, 2017). Between 2015 and 2017, around 3,000 more teachers were leaving the profession than were joining it. Teacher vacancies are rising (Foster, 2019). The teacher labour market in Australia is in oversupply, except in a few specialist areas in both primary and secondary schools, and in rural areas (McKenzie et al, 2014; Johnson et al, 2019; White, 2019). At the time of writing this book, there was little evidence to confirm the actual levels of attrition in the teacher profession. It is anticipated that the Australian Teacher Workforce Data reports to be produced by AITSL may address this gap. Noting the lack of robust evidence, Weldon (2018) draws on available research in recent years to estimate that between 25 per cent and 30 per cent of employed teachers leave the profession. On this basis, he claims that '100 graduating students would yield 49–60 teachers still teaching after five years' but if the 'wastage' figures are more like 40–50 per cent, as other researchers suggest, 'then 35–48 of 100 graduating students would still be teaching after five years' (Weldon, 2018, p 70).

Recruitment and retention 'crises' come and go in teaching. They are affected by the economic cycle, pay levels and the relative availability and attractiveness of other jobs, as well as operational issues such as how easy it is to find and pay for initial training, and how well supported teachers are in the early stages of their careers. Recruitment and retention problems do not in themselves indicate that anything is wrong with teaching as a profession. But in this current case they do. In England, qualitative research commissioned by the government showed that workload was the most important factor influencing teachers to leave the profession. As well as making suggestions for better in-school support and working conditions, teachers in this study made multiple proposals for reducing workload, and pointed to the need for greater professional recognition and greater autonomy (CooperGibson Research, 2018). Teachers say they are leaving partly because their jobs have become too much about complying with mandated practices, driving children towards test success and generating data and performances, and too little about using their professional skills, insights and judgements to help children learn (Allen and Sims, 2018). The situation is not dissimilar in Australia, where heavy 'workloads' and 'insufficient recognition or reward' contribute to teacher attrition (McKenzie et al, 2014, p 104). Increased administrative tasks, increased levels of accountability, and the burden of 'waves of "reform" and initiatives' were identified as contextual issues that contributed to attrition in a number of studies reported by Mason and Matas (2015, p 57).

Box 5.2: Dreamfields: improving test scores versus being creative in the classroom

Burn-out was common among teachers at Dreamfields, who reported 'ridiculously high' workloads and extended working hours (p 121). According to one teacher, working there was more akin to meeting sales targets than working with human beings. The formation of academies such as Dreamfields offered freedom from local authorities and the potential for more creative innovation. However, they are still judged against the same national performance indicators as other schools. Teachers at Dreamfields reported being instructed by their line managers to be more creative with lessons. However, they were also required to adhere to strict norms that allowed little room for creativity and were under intense pressure to improve examination results. The performance of their students was continually measured, ranked and tracked. If test results fell below set progression indicators, teachers expected management to 'step up' their monitoring, including meetings where they were required to explain why individual students had fallen below expectations, and there was likely to also be an increase in lesson observations and checking by senior managers.

Overall then, the evidence presented in this chapter suggests that although teachers and school leaders in our countries are working some of the longest hours among teachers worldwide, this extra effort is being misdirected. They are spending too much of their time on the wrong things. By 'wrong' we mean tasks that fail to make education better and fairer, that undermine what it means to be a teacher or school leader, and that make it less likely that teachers will be attracted into the profession and stay in it. This really matters. Teachers are *the* essential ingredient and the primary cost in any education system. Hundreds if not thousands of studies point to the vital importance of the quality of teaching, particularly in circumstances where children rely on teachers and schools most. So, if what is happening to the teaching profession is not contributing to higher-quality teaching, we have a major problem.

Combined with the problems we pointed to in Chapters 3 and 4 – too many tests and divided school systems that work for some people much better than for others – we take this as further evidence that our education systems need to change. However, as we argued in Chapter 1, we are unlikely to be able to change this situation unless there is some collective understanding of how and why we have arrived at this point. That's where we turn next – setting out the five big policy mistakes or omissions that have, together, created the situation we are in now.

6

Mistake #1: turning to the market

The first policy move we describe as a mistake is the decision to rely increasingly on a market model of school provision. By this we mean a suite of changes including expanding the range of non-state providers, making schools self-managing, requiring them to compete for students and funding, and encouraging and enabling parents to choose schools.

Many countries have moved in this direction to a greater or lesser extent in recent decades. The results are rarely free markets. High levels of state management, subsidy and regulation limit market activity. So economists tend to call markets for schooling 'quasi-markets'. But they still differ substantially from fully state-run models, where governments provide schools, employ teachers and allocate places.

In this chapter, we briefly describe the different paths towards marketisation that governments in England and Australia have taken, and the rationales for these changes. We also review evidence of policy effects, concentrating on markets themselves rather than on the mechanisms that have sprung up to govern them (such as performance measures), which we cover in Chapter 7.

Turning to the market

Marketising policies in England and Australia started from different points but have evolved in similar ways.

In Australia, the ascendency of choice as the driver of education markets is somewhat ironically linked to a social-democratic moment in policy making. The Whitlam government (1972–75) overcame an ideological objection to providing state aid to non-government schools in order to support severely under-resourced schools, mainly Catholic parish schools. Whitlam established the Schools Commission that set about classifying schools according to need. The commission did not recommend funding already adequately resourced schools but the compromises that allowed the bill to pass through parliament enabled all schools, even elite private schools, to receive some government funding. This moment was the trigger for subsequent governments, especially the conservative Howard government (1996–2007) to provide funding to non-government schools to increase their number and accessibility. Support for non-government schools has recently received an increased injection of funding by the conservative Morrison government. Since being elected in 2018, it has created a $3.4 billion 'choice and accessibility fund', as well as a special $1.2 billion fund for private schools, which is paid directly to Catholic and independent school authorities to distribute as they see fit.

The first Australian state to unleash competition as a means of driving choice and improving quality was the Kennett government in Victoria in the early 1990s. Similar to Charter Schools in the US, Kennett's Schools of the Future programme provided more autonomy and independence to government schools, including responsibility and accountability for spending their own budget and responsibility over their own staffing, while also being held more accountable for their students' achievements through learning standards (Caldwell and Hayward, 1998). However, these reforms included severe cuts in education spending achieved by closing schools and reducing teacher numbers – moves that were met with strong protests from highly unionised teaching workforces across the nation. The unpopularity of the Victorian reforms, in combination with a long period of Labor at the federal level (1983–96), worked against the creation of league tables in Australia and their marketising effects. It was not until the introduction of NAPLAN in 2008 and the creation of the MySchool website in 2010 that a national mechanism was created for assessing student performance and comparing schools, respectively. These initiatives of the Rudd/Gillard

Labor government illustrated increased marketising influences on Labor's education policies.

Independent Public Schools (IPSs) have been established for some time in Western Australia. In 2014, the Australian government funded a $70 million initiative to establish an additional 1,500 such schools across Australia. These government schools remain in the state education system, but they have greater autonomy in decision making (for example, staffing, professional development, curriculum), and more accountability. They must seek support from the local community to change their status and for the school's operational performance.

England, meanwhile, arguably had a less 'private' system to begin with, since the post-war settlement that established the education system incorporated most faith and grammar schools within the government-funded and regulated system. But this state school system has been radically transformed in the past three decades by governments of different political persuasions.

The first major shift came with the Conservatives' Education Reform Act (ERA) in 1988. This introduced school-based financial management with funding linked to pupil numbers, and encouraged autonomy and diversity through the introduction of grant-maintained schools, which were outside local authority control. 'Specialist' schools were introduced in 1994. Labour governments from 1997 to 2010 extended market reforms. In 2001, they introduced city academies, independent state schools with private sponsors (hence 'sponsored academies'), to replace 'failing schools' in disadvantaged areas. In 2006, they passed the Education and Inspections Act, which opened the door for every school to be run by a self-governing trust or foundation. When the Conservatives came back to power in 2010 in the coalition government, they pushed the door wide open. The small-scale academies programme was extended to outstanding or good schools (known as 'converter' academies), with the intention that all schools should eventually be academies. New 'free schools' were allowed to set up, and central regulations and guidance were removed to allow schools more freedom over curriculum, hours of learning and teachers' pay and conditions. By January 2019, 75 per cent of secondary and 32 per cent of primary schools were academies, and there were about 370 free schools. Chains of academies have replaced local authorities as the main providers of schools. They develop their own ethos, methods and branding; buy and sell services; train teachers; and engage in mergers and acquisitions. Mortimore (2013, p 176) argues that these marketising changes have 'fragmented' what was a 'reasonable system'; Lawn (2013a, p 231) that England now has a 'systemless system'.

Policy rationales

These changes are not the product of a single policy idea. They have had multiple interacting rationales.

Probably the major theme is the principle of choice — that parents and children (poor as well as rich) should be able to select a school that suits them. This requires diversity in the system, so that a genuine choice can be made, as well as access to a selection of schools. In England, the Citizen's Charter of 1991, followed by a Parents' Charter, were significant developments that emphasised the importance of publicly available information to enable consumer choice and accountability across public services. In Australia, the government funding of non-government schools and in England the government funding of faith, single-sex, specialist and free schools has financially underwritten what are increasingly regarded as the 'rights' of parents to choose to choose the 'right' school; a process that Proctor (2011) has argued 'has become a staple of the parenting conversation'.

But increasing choice for parents has not been the only argument for market reforms. According to the key architects of the Victorian government's Schools of the Future programme (Victoria, Directorate of School Education, 1993), increasing choice through the removal of school boundaries (de-zoning) unleashes competition (Caldwell and Spinks, 1988). Markets, they argued, should not be blamed for parents with the means and motive making schooling choices, because they would do this anyway. But the ability to choose increased the stakes and importance of school reform and the need to improve all schools so that they are the kinds of places parents want to send their children. So, the logic goes, competition forces schools to continually try to improve, and allows new providers to come in and offer something better. Making schools autonomous encourages innovation because new providers with different ideas can be attracted, because schools have to innovate to survive, and because school leaders are freed from bureaucratic requirements. And operating schools as businesses (and sometimes by businesses) makes them more efficient.

Thus Conservative education secretary Kenneth Baker argued that the 1988 reforms would weaken the power of teacher unions and local authorities, which (he claimed) were failing to improve standards and protecting weak schools and teachers. Competition would 'open it all up and it would lead to the poorer schools literally having to close' (Baker, cited in Davies, 1999, p 2). Similarly, when introducing academies over a decade later, the Labour government argued that academies would 'raise standards by innovative approaches to management, governance, teaching and the curriculum' (DfEE, 2001). Extending choice in 2005, Labour insisted that greater autonomy and 'new dynamism and providers' would free schools up to 'innovate and succeed' (DfES, 2005, p 8). In 2010 the coalition's key argument for extending academies across the whole system was that to keep up with international competitors, England had to shift power 'to the front line' (DfE, 2010, p 3). In Australia, the shift towards school-based management came from both the Right and Left in response to the perceived failings of a system centralised at the state level and broader criticisms of the bureaucratic public sector (Considine, 2012). In extending IPSs, the Australian government argued that this would 'lead to higher productivity, better quality education outcomes for students', as *The Coalition's Policy for Schools: Students First* (Abbott, 2013, p 10) expressed it.

In the context of this book, it is particularly notable that architects of market reforms have also explicitly made the case that they would make schooling fairer as well as better. Kenneth Baker acknowledged that his reforms would reintroduce selection and stratification through increased diversity and choice, but he also argued that his changes would bring benefits to the least advantaged. A visit to the Bronx in New York, where he saw great teaching overcoming social disadvantage, convinced him that there would be particular benefits for children in the poorest areas. In introducing academies, Labour said it would 'raise achievement in areas of historic underperformance' and 'transform the education of children in areas of disadvantage and need'. It would bring the greatest benefits to poorer children as their schools would be transformed and increased choice would create a system 'designed around the needs of the individual' (DfES, 2005, p 8).

Consequences: better and fairer?

These claims are not, overall, supported by the accumulated evidence. Top-line findings on academies in England are now relatively well known. There was a discernible improvement in the performance of pupils attending the earliest academies (although results were worse in nearly a third of schools), but the roll-out of the scheme has not improved schools more broadly (Eyles et al, 2016; Andrews and Perera, 2017). Wider and more detailed evidence helps explain why.

A clear problem is that school choice facilitates social sorting. Qualitative research in both Australia and England shows that middle-class parents are more likely to exercise choice towards high-attaining schools (Ball, 2003a; Vincent et al, 2010; Jackson and Lamb, 2016), and that school choices reflect perceptions of the desirability of social class and ethnic diversity as parents seek schools with 'nice children' and to avoid 'the rabble' (Byrne and Tona, 2014). Quantitatively, Burgess and colleagues (2006) demonstrated that poorer children in England are less likely to travel out of their area to better schools and Allen (2007) showed that an imaginary situation in which all children were allocated to their nearest school would produce a less socially segregated outcome. In Australia, Lamb and colleagues (2015) show that market reforms have resulted in increased enrolment in middle and high SES schools, while in low SES schools enrolment has decreased – students with higher prior attainment are bypassing their local school to attend a middle or high SES school further afield.

This does not mean that choice is the only cause of social segregation between schools. In fact, in England, large-scale studies examining segregation over time tend to show little change since the introduction of market reforms (Goldstein and Noden, 2003; Gorard et al, 2003, 2013; Cheng and Gorard, 2010; Gorard, 2014). Social sorting in the school system was already happening before the reforms of 1988, as of course was residential sorting – a key factor in a system where admissions criteria usually include closeness to school. So in many parts of the country, with stable school hierarchies and populations, marketisation might have had little effect on who goes where. However, effects can be much greater in densely populated and disadvantaged urban areas with many schools and more volatility in school performance and fortunes.

Such localised effects may not show up in country-wide studies of social segregation (Thomson and Lupton, 2017). But they really matter for the schools and students concerned. Many people worry about social segregation in the school system because of its socially divisive effects. They argue that a school system where children of all social and ethnic backgrounds mix and learn together is much more likely to produce a fair and equal society than one where they are separated. But apart from that, social segregation can produce differences in the quality of education that students receive. 'Residualised' or 'bottom of the market' schools with dwindling funds struggle to recruit teachers, run a wide variety of courses and provide material, cultural and social resources for students.

As Lamb (2007) has described in Australia, market reforms have left poorer schools 'drained of students and resources, exposed to greater gaps in academic achievement and confronted with closures or consolidation' (p 685), leaving them with 'much higher concentrations of the various groups of disadvantaged students that have the most difficult and demanding learning needs' (p 696). The drain-off of students is not only towards an increasingly large non-government sector, but also towards more desirable schools in a differentiated government system. The main lever available to other government schools to engage in competition is to increase their distinctiveness by restricting entry to selective streams or curriculum intensification in areas such as sports, dramatic arts, languages and so on.

Box 6.1: Northwest College: struggling to compete

Jackson and Lamb (2016) describe Northwest College as 'a struggling government school situated in a low-income working-class area' (p 5). The college is characterised by its socioeconomic disadvantage and vulnerability to being perceived as a 'losing' school. Its students are drawn disproportionately from the lower range of the achievement spectrum. In most NAPLAN domains, results are consistently 'below' or 'substantially below' the national average. In an effort to rebrand itself, and to attract higher-achieving students, the college has adopted a university preparation programme, with the goal of improving the number of students who gain university entrance and, in turn, increasing enrolments in the school and relieving the additional challenges associated with smaller school size, such as limitations on curriculum breadth and student support services (Lamb, 2007). Jackson and Lamb (2016) describe a 'striking difference' between Northwest's resources and those of another school in their study, Southeast School, 'a high-achieving private school situated in a desirable suburb' (p 5), positioned at the other end of the educational marketplace. The per-student income from different sources – mainly state funding for Northwest and lesser amounts of federal funding than Southeast School whose main income is from school fees – combine such that 'Northwest College received a little over half the income per student for Southeast School until 2012, when an increase in government funding raised this to almost two-thirds' (p 8). Consequently, Northwest is not only attempting to meet the needs of students with deeper learning needs than Southeast, but it must do so with fewer resources.

So governments that want to have, or are stuck with, systems designed around the principle of choice must always take remedial measures to try to minimise inequitable outcomes. Such measures include extra funding to schools in challenging areas, regulation of admissions rules, choice advisers to support less advantaged parents, and so on. As described earlier in the chapter, they may also call on market principles themselves to sort out the problems: competition between schools to drive standards up across the board so no one has to go to a bad school, and giving schools freedom to innovate, improve and meet local needs.

Nor is the evidence in favour of competition and autonomy very favourable. There is *some* evidence that competition can lead to improvement in test results for schools that need to compete. In England, schools that changed from local authority control to more autonomous forms (grant maintained schools in the 1990s, and academies in the 2000s and 2010s) did tend to see improvements in results, although they also changed their intakes, having a smaller proportion of disadvantaged or lower-attaining students (Allen, 2010; Wilson, 2011; Andrews and Perera, 2017). Gibbons and colleagues (2008) found evidence of greater improvement for schools with more competitors. So competition may cause schools to 'up their game' in order to survive in an environment where funding depends on student numbers and performance on high-level measures. The problem is that the behaviour in which schools have to engage in order to become more competitive has a tendency to make schooling less fair. When schools are required to sell themselves to prospective parents and students, they tend be more focused on performance measures, inspection outcomes and other visible signs of their value, and less keen to admit or retain children and young people who do not make a positive contribution to performance. School leaders must prioritise succeeding in the competition for students, reputation, resources and survival, and this means that some students will be much more valuable (and valued) than others. Ball describes 'an increased, often predominant orientation towards the internal wellbeing of the institution and its members and a shift away from concern with more general social and educational issues within "the community"' (Ball, 2017, p 54).

This affects who is admitted to schools, as schools choose children. In England, schools with autonomy over their admissions arrangements have also been shown to flout the Admissions Code, which is supposed to ensure fair admissions. Practices include failing to prioritise children in the care of the local authority or with SEN, and asking for too much information from parents such as parental birth certificates or first language (Academies Commission, 2013; British Humanist Association and Fair Admissions Campaign, 2015; Rayner, 2017). In Australia, similar concerns have been raised by Holloway and Keddie (2020, p 786), who argue that increased principal autonomy 'sometimes occurs at the expense of fracturing the cohesion of the greater public education system'. It also affects practices within schools, including the narrowing of curriculum, focus on testing, and exclusions and 'off-rolling' as described in Chapters 3 and 4, as well as the changes in teachers' work described in Chapter 5. Courtney and Gunter (2015, pp 400, 407) describe 'relentless leadership' with corporate-style demands for compliance and threats of 'consequences'. Liu and colleagues (2020) found that not only were schools less likely to admit children with SEN once they became a sponsored academy, but changing to an academy also resulted in a higher proportion of students being declassified as needing SEN support.

Box 6.2: Parkside Academy: market pressures and the homogenisation of practice

When Parkside Academy was set up it had a more challenging intake than other secondary schools serving the area, referred to as Green End, and was regarded as the bottom school in an established local 'hierarchy of desirability' (Salokangas and Ainscow, 2018, p 22). Parkside's student population was skewed towards those experiencing the highest levels of deprivation, drawn almost exclusively from the immediate locality. It tended to include parents who did not exercise a choice through local authority admissions procedures, and children who did not get places at other 'more desirable' schools. Data at that time also revealed distinct patterns in school populations in Green End, with a faith school catering predominantly for White and African Caribbean learners, and three single-sex schools catering for White and Asian learners; Parkside's population was much more ethnically diverse. One parent explained these patterns as resulting from particular groups of parents choosing to send their children to schools where, in the light of growing inter-ethnic tensions within the district, 'they thought they would be safe' (p 22). Competition to attract 'good' students, and to be seen as academically successful (and thus 'desirable') led to secondary schools in the area having very similar approaches – strict, formal, teaching from the front of the class. The lack of diversity among the schools' approaches to learning was seen as a factor perpetuating the exclusion of certain groups, and the unwillingness of some learners/families to engage with schooling.

So it is not particularly surprising that improvements in results when greater competition is introduced are not evenly shared. In England, Machin and Silva's (2013) analysis of the academies programme showed that all the gains were made by students with medium to high prior attainment. Effects of academy conversion, they write, were 'insignificantly different from zero – and possibly negative for later conversions – in the bottom 10% and 20% of the ability distribution' (p 99). McNally (2015) notes that since students from disadvantaged backgrounds are more likely to be found in the lower prior attainment groups 'one might infer that the policy was not particularly effective for improving the attainment of disadvantaged students' (p 65). And when Hutchings and colleagues (2015) looked at the effects of academy chains, investigating the government's claim that these were the 'best way of working to improve the performance of previously struggling schools and the educational outcomes of their often disadvantaged pupils' (p 4), they found that while some chains had achieved impressive outcomes for disadvantaged students, a large group had results that were not improving. Moreover, differences in performance were growing over time.

Similar unpromising results were found in Western Australia's experiment with IPSs, which, as previously noted, has been extended to other states. An evaluation commissioned by the state's Department of Education found 'no evidence to indicate changes in enrolments or student achievement.' (Centre for Program Evaluation and Shelby Consulting, 2013. p 72). There are some good news stories of the ways in which schools have utilised IPS funding, including to reorganise and renew the culture of a school, which in turn enabled the school to 'win back [our] reputation' (Fitzgerald et al, 2018), and to redirect funding to ensure that the needs of disadvantaged learners were adequately resourced and addressed (Keddie, 2016). But evidence of improvements in student performance in IPSs is equivocal at best. And these 'gains' come at a cost: in the education marketplace, schools are in competition for staff recruitment and student enrolments. One set of schools accumulates advantages over others (Centre for Program Evaluation and Shelby Consulting, 2013, p 6); equity and diversity are undermined; and, the process of residualisation continues unencumbered, leaving the least well-resourced schools with higher concentrations of disadvantaged students (Keddie, 2016; Fitzgerald et al, 2018).

Turning to the broader effects of autonomy – on innovation, efficiency or democracy – the evidence is more mixed, probably because autonomy has taken different forms and been introduced for different reasons. Pushing more decisions to the school level does not have to be about marketisation, it can also be about delivering more say to local communities and to local leaders. The work of school leaders is an important mediating factor on student achievement. School leaders who are able to mobilise staff selection, high-quality professional development and appraisal; set priorities based on student performance; and establish a shared purpose have been shown to succeed when operating in low SES contexts (Caldwell, 2016). In the US, Charter Schools following a long school day and behavioural 'no excuses' model have also been shown to increase academic achievement (Eyles et al, 2016).

The trouble is that getting the right amount of autonomy, used in the right ways, is hard to achieve. In England, a DfE survey of academies (Cirin, 2014) showed that they *were* using their management freedoms. For example, 87 per cent were directly procuring services formally provided by local authorities; 60 per cent were collaborating more formally with other schools; 56 per cent had changed performance management systems for teachers and 48 per cent had added new non-teaching positions. Fifty-five per cent had also changed their curriculum. However, in-depth research in schools suggests that autonomous schools do not always use the freedoms they have to change what goes on in the classroom. Salokangas and Ainscow (2018) concluded from their study of Parkside Academy that ironically the apparatus set up to manage a marketised system (standardised performance measures and inspections) constrains autonomy and innovation in teaching and the curriculum. Mechanisms and incentives to collaborate with other local schools to support innovation and share good practice were also weakened by making schools independent of local authorities. So marketisation can deter innovation rather than enable it. Similarly, market pressures may constrain any benefits that autonomy may theoretically have for closer engagement with parents and communities, as schools position parents as consumers, customers and clients, rather than as civic actors and initiators who could legitimately influence schools' work (Ralls, 2019).

The recent English experience of moving very quickly to a system where most schools are autonomous also suggests that autonomy can produce efficiency, but it does not necessarily do so. Schools must procure their own goods and services. Recent evidence suggests that academies spend less on running costs – and more on teaching staff – than local authority schools. But inefficiencies are created when they operate on their own or in small trusts, or when geographically distant from partner schools (Andrews and Townley, 2017). There are issues with oversight and accountability for public funds, for example, excessively high levels of executive pay; purchasing of goods and services from companies personally associated with school leaders; and weak finance, audit and governance systems (Greany and Scott, 2014; Syal, 2014; ESFA, 2019). A study of commercialisation in NSW public schools showed increasing levels of commercialisation as central departments evacuated the provision of professional development and other services (Lingard et al, 2017). Interestingly, 'the commercial providers were augmenting the interventions and directions that departments were setting and/or signalling as vitally important to schools and school leaders' (p 18), suggesting a more complex relationship that was not limited to commercial providers replacing services previously provided by departments.

Overall, then, the evidence from England and Australia matches what the OECD found in 2010 when it conducted a major review of the effects of markets in schooling: marketisation has very little, if any, positive effect on educational outcomes (Waslander et al, 2010). The impact on equity is heavily dependent on local context, but there is rarely any evidence of desegregation and parents around the world exercise choices in ways that decrease rather than increase equity. Turning to the market to improve education has made it neither better nor fairer. It has been a costly mistake.

7

Mistake #2: letting test scores drive policy

The second policy move that we describe as a mistake is the over-focus in the education system on producing ever higher test scores.

Test scores should have a place in education policy. They can tell us about what is being achieved and how it matches up to what our societies and economies need from schooling. They can highlight groups of students who are doing less well out of the system and indicate where extra investment is needed. They can inform decisions about the effectiveness of different educational practices and help teachers to work effectively. Most people also acknowledge that students' scores can also serve useful purposes in holding schools to account, representing the interests of children, young people, parents and communities and ensuring that public money is being spent well and wisely.

However, over recent decades, test scores have come to dominate education policy decisions. They have become the reasoning arguments or 'logos' of educational policy making, in a shift described by policy sociologist Professor Bob Lingard as 'policy as numbers' (Lingard, 2011, p 356). In this chapter, we trace this shift in England and Australia. We explain why it has come about and why the evidence demonstrates that it is a mistake.

'Policy as numbers' in England and Australia

In his key book on education policy, *The Education Debate* (Ball, 2017), Professor Stephen Ball identifies the start of the 'policy as numbers' phenomenon in England in the creation of the government's Assessment of Performance Unit (APU) in 1975. APU was tasked with developing methods of assessing and monitoring achievement and identifying the incidence of underachievement – a controversial move at the time as it was seen to erode teachers' responsibility for curriculum development and assessment. But it was the 1988 ERA that gave tests and their outcomes a much more central role in education policy. ERA established the national curriculum and its SATs. In Australia, this move to a national curriculum and assessment programme came in 2008 with the establishment of NAPLAN. Prior to this, states and territories conducted literacy and numeracy testing programmes for all students in at least Years 3 and 5, but results were not used for the purpose of comparing schools – not publicly at least. The first national survey of English literacy was conducted in 1996 partly to develop national benchmarks for assessing the effectiveness of approaches to the teaching of literacy (Masters and Forster, 1997). Still, it would be over a decade until NAPLAN was introduced.

Our focus in this chapter is not the tests themselves and the many arguments that rage about how many tests there should be, at what age, who should administer them, what form they should take and so on. Rather, it is on how test results are used in policy making and in the management of the education system.

In England, since 1997, test data have been used to set national attainment targets that have become the central objectives of education policy, on which ministers have staked their reputations and jobs. Targets have been cascaded to individual schools, along with sanctions for not meeting them. An early example was the Labour government's 2008 'National Challenge', which 'named and shamed' all secondary schools not meeting a threshold of 30 per cent of students achieving five or more GCSE or equivalent passes at grades A*–C including English and maths. It set a target that no school would drop below that level in three years' time. New funds were linked to the development of 'turnaround' plans, such as becoming an academy or joining with another school (Bolton, 2010). Similar, but higher, floor targets have been retained by subsequent governments, and from 2016 these were extended to define 'coasting schools' (based on thresholds of achievement and progress measures) that could also be subject to intervention. Underpinning these developments has been the development of increasingly sophisticated datasets (particularly the National Pupil Database [NPD] established in 2002) and analytic capacity. Since 2016, for example, schools have been accountable for pupil progress throughout the school career, based on prior attainment. Attainment data are a key part of Ofsted inspection, increasingly so during the 2000s and early 2010s, although their use was diminished in the 2019 inspection framework amid concerns that they had too much of an influence on school practice.

In Australia, similarly, NAPLAN data are used to support targets or benchmarking in national policy, in this case informing national agreements between the Australian government and all states and territories. The availability of national comparative data has resulted in a major change in the nature of Commonwealth–state funding arrangements. States and territories now agree to delivering outputs and outcomes in exchange for 'incentive payments' that are intended to drive reforms (COAG, 2007, p 1). The distribution of federal government financial resources is 'now explicitly tied to various forms of compliance and to demonstrable gains in standardised measurable performance' (Comber, 2012, p 123). However, while a unique student identifier (USI) is currently being considered as a means of sharing student education records across systems and jurisdictions, Australia has not yet developed a national student database in the way that England has. The National Schools Interoperability Program, agreed by all systems across the nation, is a step in this direction because it will provide essential data infrastructure to enable interoperability of school data (Sellar, 2017).

Test data are, of course, also crucial in the operation of school markets, to provide information to parents and others about school outcomes. In England, secondary schools have had to publish their exam results since 1981 and since 1992 governments have produced 'performance tables'. This means that parents can compare schools on their raw examination results and also, over time, on a varying array of additional measures: value-added scores, progress measures, measures of attainment for different groups of students and the size of gaps. Australia has followed a similar pathway. NAPLAN results have been made public through the MySchool website since 2010. The published results compare the test performance of students in Years 3, 5, 7, and 9 in each school with the performance of students nationally. It also enables comparison with statistically similar schools, on an Index of Community and Socio-Educational Advantage (ICSEA) and includes a summary of demographic and financial data for each school. These data are represented in the form of cohort gains over two years compared with students with the same starting point and similar backgrounds. Currently, the information is not used to rank or label schools by national or state jurisdictions but each year when NAPLAN results are made available, the media engages in a form of comparative commentary intended to produce this kind of effect. It is because of the high consequences for schools as well as for students that these standardised tests are often described as 'high-stakes' tests.

Policy drivers

Scholars studying these changes have identified two main drivers of the increasing use of test scores in shaping education policy and practice.

The first is the increasing importance given to the economic purposes of education – building the so-called 'human capital' that can support economic growth and international competitiveness. In England, it is commonly acknowledged that the turning point in thinking about education in this way was Prime Minister James Callaghan's Ruskin College speech of 1976, in which he argued that the balance of education had tipped too much away from preparing young people for work and that this had to change in a world where jobs were demanding higher skill levels. This same message has been reiterated over and over in multiple policy texts and speeches, emphasising the necessity and urgency of educational reform and rising standards (Ball, 2017). In Australia, at the national level, the need to link 'education and training programs more closely to the current needs of the labour market and to future employment opportunities' was strongly articulated in the report on employment and growth *Working Nation: Policies and Programs* (Keating, 1994, p 89). It was not the first time these concerns had been expressed but it was the first time a significant amount of money, approximately $3 million, was allocated to collect, reliable national data on the literacy levels of school students at three significant stages of schooling (Masters and Forster, 1997).

The economic purpose of schooling is a global policy discourse, made more urgent by the globalisation of trade and labour, and reinforced by the growing availability (principally through the OECD) of comparable data about education systems and outcomes in competitor countries (Lawn, 2013b). Since 2003, the OECD's PISA league tables have enabled countries to benchmark themselves on measures of reading, mathematics and scientific literacy. Every three years they provide 'PISA shocks' (Baroutsis and Lingard, 2018) to countries that have been overtaken or are struggling, while valorising the policies of those that have boosted their league table position. Many countries have adopted PISA-like assessments and begun to scrutinise or copy the practices of countries whose students consistently perform well in PISA results, resulting in some policy convergence.

The second driver is a change in the way that education systems are managed, making them more reliant on high-level indicators. Many writers on this topic emphasise the introduction and evolution of the new public management (NPM) that accompanied marketisation from the 1980s (see, for example, Gunter et al, 2016). Others describe a shift from 'government' to 'governance', as public services are no longer provided directly by lower tiers of state bureaucracies but by multiple state, private and charitable organisations that governments steer at a distance by mandating outcomes and using targets, incentives and sanctions (Ozga, 2009). Both in England and Australia the increasing centralisation of education policy described in Chapter 2 has also demanded new technologies for direction and surveillance over lower tiers. *Guardian* journalist Fiona Millar (2016) reports that at the time of the Ruskin speech, the English Secretary of State for schools had just three powers over schools – 40 years later she had more than 2,500.

Particularly influential, initially in England but later globally, was the 'deliverology' approach developed by Sir Michael Barber – Head of New Labour's Standards and Effectiveness Unit and Prime Minister's Delivery Unit in the late 1990s–early 2000s. 'Deliverology' was a systematic approach to system-wide improvement based on target setting, monitoring, tight performance review, rewards and sanctions (Barber et al, 2010; Gewirtz et al, 2019). However, even subsequent governments eschewing such command and control approaches have retained and even intensified the use of targets and performance data to manage and regulate autonomous systems.

Just as in the case of markets, it is striking how politicians have often justified the emphasis on attainment data and targets as an approach designed to reduce educational inequalities – both in terms of access and outcomes. As labour markets and job demands have changed, and entry-level positions with few qualifications all but vanished, it has been seen as increasingly imperative to level up the distribution of human capital, to avoid entrenching social class divides. And as efforts have been made to improve schools, setting targets for the lowest-attaining schools has been labelled as a strategy to promote greater equity, making sure that the most disadvantaged students are not served by the least good schools, nor overlooked within schools. In the early 2000s, the UK Labour government described its floor targets as setting universal entitlements – 'the social equivalent of the minimum wage' (Neighbourhood Renewal Unit, 2008). Under the current Conservative government, schools are required to report on attainment and progress for different groups of pupils, and receive per capita funding for each disadvantaged pupil to be spent on raising their attainment and closing attainment gaps. In theory at least, such measures keep the spotlight on the least advantaged students and make success for them central to the idea of what it means to be a good school (Francis et al, 2017c). The contrasting situation in Australia is described in Chapter 9. Suffice to say here that successive Australian governments, both Labor and Liberal, have failed to fund Australian schools based on need, yet both identify improving the academic achievement of all students, including priority equity cohorts, as central to their education policies.

Consequences: better and fairer?

So has this focus on raising test scores made education better and fairer?

This is a difficult question to answer, partly because, in quantitative studies, it is hard to isolate the effects of focusing on tests when multiple aspects of education policy are changing at the same time. That is one reason why a study by economist Professor Simon Burgess and colleagues at Bristol University has received a lot of attention. Burgess and colleagues (2011) examined what happened when Wales stopped publishing school performance tables, while England did not, while other elements of school accountability systems remained the same. They found 'significant and robust evidence' (Burgess et al, 2011, p 1) that Wales' removal of the tables had reduced school effectiveness, measured by student achievement. Moreover, it was lower-attaining and poorer students who have lost out through the changes, in contrast to findings of similar studies from the US.

There is also some evidence that when achievement gaps are highlighted, students who might previously have gone 'under the radar' receive more attention. Reports from English schools in recent years demonstrate that when required to report on disadvantage gaps and given additional ring-fenced money, schools did identify these students and make bespoke plans for them (Ofsted, 2013, 2014). Similarly, OECD's reporting of PISA results, which consistently promotes high achievement and equitable learning outcomes as equally important and simultaneously achievable objectives, has allowed participating nations to better understand the influence of SES and student ethnicity, as well as school and regional ethnic diversity on student achievement within their own contexts (Schnepf and Volante, 2018).

It is important to look beyond this kind of evidence, however. Test scores are only one (narrow) concept of 'better' education, so asking 'Does focusing on test scores improve test scores?' is not the same as asking 'Does focusing on test scores improve education?' To fully understand the effects of the 'policy as numbers' approach, we need to understand its impact on educational *practice* – what is actually happening to teaching and learning when policies change.

Studies that take this approach tend to produce consistent and worrying findings. A key point is that teachers understand the stakes involved in so-called high-stakes testing. In Australia, the official purposes of NAPLAN, as indicated by ACARA (2019b), are to provide information about how individual students perform, how education programmes are working, and areas that need to be improved. However, when Polesel and colleagues (2014) conducted their major study of over 8000 educators, they found that, according to participants, the most commonly cited purpose of NAPLAN was as a school-ranking tool. The majority of respondents also ranked highly NAPLAN's use as a policing tool, and both of these purposes were ranked more highly than the official ones. More than 90 per cent of respondents indicated that lower than expected results on NAPLAN would mean that a school would have trouble attracting and retaining students.

As a result, educators change what they do. And why wouldn't they? As Amanda Spielman, England's Chief Inspector, said: 'We have a highly transparent system and performance data is valuable for many purposes, including holding schools to account. But most of us, if told our job depends on clearing a particular bar, will try to give ourselves the best chance of securing that outcome' (Spielman, 2017).

A 'logic of numbers' therefore takes over (Hardy, 2015, p 350). Hardy's research on the effects of NAPLAN showed that 'over a short period of time, a test-centric focus has become increasingly evident' (2015, p 335). Practices included increasing repeated test preparation and grouping children into reading groups from very early ages, which had negative effects on those in lower groups because they had fewer opportunities for rich and varied learning experiences and resources.

In England, Gewirtz and colleagues (2019) analysed open-ended responses to a survey from over 1,800 secondary school teachers to learn about how they were responding to the new Progress 8 measure. Although this measure should in theory mean that teachers give equal attention to the progress of all students, in practice teachers reported becoming less able to respond in tailored ways to individual needs because of pressures to focus on enhancing school results. Curriculum was narrowed,

Box 7.1: Waterwell Primary School: the effects of standardised tests on teaching and teachers

Within a year of NAPLAN being introduced, in Waterwell Primary School, which was in no way a 'test-shy community' (Comber, 2012, p 120), Comber witnessed substantial changes in practice, such as excluding students from testing in order to maintain the school's results and jettisoning established successful practices and curriculum areas in order to prepare students for the format and expectations of tests. They also spent substantial extra time planning and executing data collection, explaining tests and results to parents and students, and balancing the messaging to these groups between NAPLAN results and teachers' own assessments of student's progress and abilities. The widely reported impact of NAPLAN on the narrowing of the curriculum and on teachers' pedagogical responsiveness was visible, but Comber's methodological device also provided insight into the less reported loss of teachers' faith and confidence in their own judgement. The dislodgement of a teacher's sense of professional capability weakens their ability to respond to students with high support needs who rely on their teachers' expertise to help them, and to have the confidence to do so. Some teachers at Waterwell reported that the emotional and professional demands of being locked into practices and goals intended to achieve short-term test results would make them leave the profession.

with creative and vocational subjects excluded. Teaching was more formulaic and transmissionist. Teachers and students were equally demotivated. As one teacher put it:

> Teaching is no longer about doing the best you can for your pupils; it's about data and numbers. Pupils are not children anymore; they are dots on a graph which must look a certain way. I am leaving teaching because of changes to teaching. I have seen teachers ignore a class because they have to hit data deadlines because that is what is important these days. (Head of year and design and technology teacher in a local authority school with a 'Good' Ofsted rating, cited in Gewirtz et al, 2019 p 17)

Significantly, teachers in this study were most concerned about the effects of these new measures, and the practices they produced, on students with additional needs and lower self-esteem, exactly the students whom the measures were supposed to benefit.

In other words, resonating with a wealth of earlier UK, Australian and international research (Lipman, 2004; Au, 2009; Berliner, 2011; Ravitch, 2011; Stobart and Eggen, 2012), the studies we cite here make it really clear that the 'logic of numbers' is a major contributor to the problems described in Chapters 3, 4 and 5. It may possibly have led to an increase in test scores, but it has made education worse rather than better and contributed to widening inequalities. As Gewirtz and colleagues (2019) put it, 'the unintended harms it generates may be outweighing its benefits' (p 1).

Box 7.2: Farrell High School: numbers getting in the way of meeting students' needs

Farrell High School was placed in 'Special Measures' by Ofsted and required to focus intensively on raising its results (Firth et al, 2014). But both the Ofsted judgement and the focus on numbers made it harder to support disadvantaged students. Being put in 'Special Measures' had serious repercussions for Farrell High's reputation and its enrolment numbers, with financial consequences leading to redundancies of teaching, support and administrative staff. The long-term effects were felt with reduced levels of in-class support, classes shared between two or more teachers and subjects taught by non-specialist teachers. Under these circumstances, teachers cannot always deliver appropriate pedagogies and the likelihood that students will experience consistent quality teaching and learning is compromised (Firth et al, 2014, p 882). This case demonstrates the negative impact of striving to close the achievement gap for students who, due to other gaps in their educational experiences such as limited resources and opportunities for learning, might be best served by improvements in the overall quality of their learning experiences. It is these very learning experiences that suffer when teachers' pedagogical responses are oriented towards improved test performance. At Farrell High, students were inclined to make choices oriented towards test achievement, 'rather than what they might do to pursue their interests, extend themselves and reach their potential' (Firth et al, 2014, p 880).

All of this is very well recognised, not just by academics and teachers and their representatives in teacher unions, but by many politicians and officials. Over ten years ago, in England, the

House of Commons Education Committee 2008 recommended decoupling tests from school accountability measures – a recommendation the government rejected. Ofsted's recent move to downplay performance data and focus on what is actually being taught is another recognition. In Australia, the Senate Employment, Education and Training References Committee, which conducted a report into the effectiveness of NAPLAN (2014), concluded that there had been 'a range of unintended consequences', including 'negative or adverse consequences such as a narrowing of the curriculum or "teaching to the test"; the creation of a NAPLAN preparation industry which compounds the perception that NAPLAN is a "high-stakes" test; and adverse or negative impacts on students' (p 13).

Yet despite this, systems of high-stakes testing remain in place, embedded in the practice of school leaders and teachers,

Long-term implications

Perhaps even more damaging is what 'policy as numbers' is doing to our understanding of what education is – the foundation for future education policy.

High academic standards are an important goal of education policy. However, as sociologist Professor Wendy Espeland has pointed out, we need to be careful not to be totally diverted by numbers. Although 'measurement can help us see complicated things in ways that make it possible to intervene in them productively (consider measures of global warming)', it can also 'narrow our appraisal of value and relevance to what can be measured easily, at the expense of other ways of knowing' (Espeland and Stevens, 2008, p 432).

In education, many things that are important '*cannot* be counted, or added, or ranked because there is no genuine unit of account' (O'Neill, 2013, p 14, emphasis in original). When we narrow our appraisal of value and relevance to achievement in tests, we take our eye off the substance of education, even within the subjects that we are testing. We 'mistake badges and stickers for learning itself' (Spielman, 2017). It becomes acceptable for curriculum to be narrowed to basic knowledge and skills that can be rehearsed in the desired test format. It becomes acceptable for children to be bored and disengaged even when we know that deeper learning and desire to learn are much better foundations for future success. We also take attention away from less measurable or immeasurable educational objectives such as physical, moral, civic and artistic development (Andrews et al, 2014), or from learning outcomes that lie outside tested subjects, including the ability to engage in problem solving, to communicate effectively, to work with a range of peers, and to write creatively and critically. As Ball points out, one of the effects of our understanding of our current situation as a 'knowledge economy' is that it has commodified knowledge and intellectual culture: 'Our understanding of the world shifts from social values created by people to a world in which everything is viewed in terms of quantities; everything is simply a sum of value realised or hoped for' (Ball, 2017, p 227).

So too much focus on numbers is not just important in the 'here and now' for children who spend hours and hours going over the same things at the expense of wider opportunities, and who are consigned to lower groups or even excluded from school. It also diminishes our collective imagination of what education is and ought to be about, and thus makes it difficult to change policy in substantial ways. Increasingly, our countries' educational policy decisions are driven not by national consensus about the nature and purpose of schooling, but by political concerns about desired achievement levels – levels set by comparisons with other countries, 'like schools' and agreed rates of development and progression. Education systems are rewarded and punished for their performance by politicians who function as 'ringmasters' (Ozga, 2009, p 151). The big questions, debates and decisions about education policy are obscured or reduced to simple questions of their effect on test scores.

Lingard (2011) therefore argues that policy as numbers is a manifestation of what Laidi describes as the reduction of contemporary politics to 'managing the ordinary present' (Laidi, 1998, p 7, cited in Lingard, 2011, p 357) – a technicist and in some sense depoliticised politics in which policy is a tool of governance and modification rather than a tool to deliver a different and more positive future. It lacks, Lingard argues, a 'horizon of expectation' (2011, p 357) or a 'progressive imaginary' (2011, p 355).

This narrowing of policy thinking is contributing to the behaviours we saw in Chapters 3, 4 and 5. It is also dangerously limiting our confidence and capacity to change education for the better. We return to these issues in Chapters 10 and 12.

8

Mistake #3: over-prescribing teachers' work

Our third mistake is the over-prescription of teachers' work.

There is no doubt that teaching is the central activity of schooling – the 'flipside' of learning. It is rightly a major focus of education policy, not just because teachers' salaries are by far the biggest budget item in school spending. The value of good teachers to children's learning is almost universally acknowledged and they are critical to the functioning of society. This was patently demonstrated during the global COVID-19 pandemic when teachers rapidly pivoted to support children learning from home, while also keeping schools open for the children of essential workers.

In the past three decades in England, and for a shorter time in Australia, the overall direction of policies to improve the quality of teaching has been to standardise both what is taught and how it is taught. These moves have had some beneficial effects, including the explicit naming of valued learning outcomes and knowledge, and the potential for the breadth and complexity of teachers' work to be identified and recognised. However, combined with the effects of market pressures and 'datafication' (Chapters 6 and 7), they have limited the professional judgement of teachers and narrowed their pedagogical repertoires so that teachers can make less difference, not more. In this chapter we explain what has happened and how the balance came to tip too far.

Prescribing teaching quality

Education in England has long been characterised by a contest for control between government, teachers and, to a certain extent, universities and their examination boards (McCulloch, 1993). The period from 1988 to 2010 saw substantial shifts in favour of government. The first major move was the introduction of the national curriculum by the Conservative government, bringing a higher degree of standardisation to what was taught. The second was the creation of Ofsted in 1992, bringing greater standardisation of practice. Ofsted replaced a variable system of Her Majesty's Inspectors and local inspection. It brought in a common inspection framework that, as we saw in Chapter 5, effectively prescribes practice in many schools as leaders attempt to create performances that will satisfy the gaze of Ofsted inspectors.

However, it was the New Labour government from 1997 that introduced a much higher level of specificity in the government prescription of classroom practice, first with the National Literacy Strategy (NLS) Framework for Teaching, which specified set minute-by-minute formats for lessons and detailed objectives for literacy teaching at different stages of primary education. The NLS and the 1999 Numeracy Strategy were subsequently rolled into the National Strategies, which covered a wider range of primary and secondary education. Large teams at DfE produced detailed guidance and resources: curriculum blocks; schemes of work; suggested lesson plans; and advice and training to schools. At the same time, Labour took steps to 'modernise' the teaching profession, introducing new standards for teacher 'training' (a discursive shift from teacher education) and practice as well as new career structures and performance-related pay (Whitty, 2000; Beck, 2009).

The return of the Conservatives to government in 2010 brought a change of direction. The National Strategies were abolished as part of a new commitment to teacher autonomy and academies were given freedom from the national curriculum as well as over teacher pay, conditions and qualifications. Much of the education and development of teachers and responsibility for school improvement was handed to teachers, with the creation of 'Teaching Schools' that could train their own teachers, and various 'Leaders of Education' roles – serving teachers and leaders charged with supporting other schools. The Chartered College of Teaching, a new professional body for teachers, was introduced in 2017 along with Chartered Teacher status. At the same time, however, the government moved towards greater standardisation of practice by pushing hard for teachers and schools to adopt practices that 'work' according to evidence from trials and experimental research. In 2011, it established the Education Endowment Foundation (EEF) to fund and disseminate research in 'what works' in raising the attainment of the poorest pupils. EEF's 'toolkits' are promoted by government as 'evidence which sets out what works and what doesn't' (DfE, 2016, p 38). Government, EEF and the Institute for Effective Education collaborate in running a research schools network that encourages schools to 'make use of evidence-based programmes and practices' (Research Schools Network, 2020). While these policies position teachers as autonomous in reviewing research and changing their practices accordingly, they rest on a particular view of teaching, in which the teacher is following or implementing a tried–and–tested instructional method, often one tightly scripted and packaged by a commercial or charitable provider. The Conservative–Liberal Democrat coalition also introduced new Teachers' Standards that 'set clear expectations about the skills that every teacher in our schools should demonstrate. They will make a significant improvement to teaching by ensuring teachers can focus on the skills that matter most' (DfE, 2011).

Teachers in Australia have long struggled to have their status and agency recognised and valued. The former highly centralised state systems of education exercised firm control over teachers' practices, monitored by inspectors and maintained by authoritarian leadership at the school level. The report *Quality of Education in Australia* (Karmel, 1985) advocated for teachers to have a more active role in setting and maintaining the standards of practice of members of the profession. Little progress was made in this regard and increasing concerns about falling literacy standards during the 1980s and 1990s shone an increasingly harsh light on the quality of the teaching profession, coinciding with a shift in emphasis in policy rationales from inputs to outputs (see the following section on policy rationales). A Senate inquiry in the late 1990s, *A Class Act*, was sympathetic towards addressing a 'serious crisis of morale amongst teachers' (Senate Employment, Education and Training References Committee, 1988, p 21). It had one main theme – to strengthen the profession, especially its role in the development of standards. Several reports followed (for example, Ramsey, 2000; DEST, 2003), and all echoed the call for a national system for professional standards and certification (Ingvarson, 2010). Initially, professional associations took up the challenge of developing standards for their specialist fields. By 2009, more than 20 professional associations had developed or were in the process of developing standards for the purpose of strengthening and supporting a self-regulated profession (Ingvarson, 2010). This intended purpose was displaced by the determination of successive federal governments to improve perceived weaknesses in teacher quality and hold the profession accountable for delivering learning outcomes. The implementation of NAPLAN in 2008 provided the mechanism for operationalising this accountability, and the release of Australian Professional Standards for Teachers (Australian Institute for Teaching and School Leadership, 2011) provided the framework for intensifying the focus on teacher quality, thus enabling a 'broader apparatus of nationalising educational practices in Australia' (Hardy, 2015, p 342).

The trajectories of policies aimed at regulating and improving perceived weaknesses in teaching quality followed different timelines in England and Australia, but they invoked similar underlying principles and operational mechanisms. In relation to concerns about reading proficiency, the National Literacy Strategy (launched in 1998) in the UK (Literacy Task Force, 1997) and *Australia's Teaching Reading Report* (DEST, 2005) demonstrated a clear 'paradigm convergence', visible also in the *Teaching Children to Read* report (National Institute of Child Health and Human Develpment, 2000) in the US. Harris and colleagues (2010) have identified a number of similarities among these documents that illustrate this convergence, including the following:

- Recommended methods are assumed to work for all children.
- There is a narrow focus on reading attainment through a set of subskills including oral language, phonemic awareness and phonics skills, vocabulary, grammar, fluency and comprehension.
- The evidence base is limited to quantitative studies.
- Experimental research conducted in psychology is valued over educational research.

Education as a field of study is associated with a rich and diverse set of research methodologies, yet the convergence illustrated in these documents reflects widespread valorisation by policy makers of a narrow set of evidence produced by quantitative studies, preferably large data sets, randomised control tests, and experimental research. In 2020, Australia followed England's example in investing in the gathering and dissemination of 'the best available evidence about effective practice in schools and early childhood settings' (Education Council, 2014). The Education Council, which is made up of ministers with portfolio responsibility for school education, higher education and/or early childhood in each Australian jurisdiction, announced it would invest $50 million over four years to establish a national evidence institute to work with teachers and researchers to:

- curate and translate evidence of what works in the classroom;
- mobilise this evidence to ensure it can be easily and freely accessed;
- generate new evidence of effective teaching and learning practices.

It remains to be seen how this new institute will function. If it follows the tendency towards convergence illustrated earlier, by relying on a limited set of evidence, it is likely that it will further narrow and standardise teachers' practices, further over-prescribing their work.

Policy rationales

These policy moves to improve teaching are not isolated initiatives. They arise from the same concerns about the need to 'drive up' and equalise 'standards' that motivated the moves to marketisation and datafication discussed in Chapters 6 and 7. They are evidently closely associated with test-driven accountability. However, distinct rationales related to the nature of teaching and how to improve it can also be identified.

In Australia, the *Quality of Education in Australia* report (Karmel, 1985) signalled a shift in the role of the national government from a focus on inputs and overcoming deficiencies in provision, towards a focus on outcomes by overcoming perceived deficiencies in teachers and their enactment of the curriculum. Emerging from a period in which national education policy was strongly focused on levelling up inputs, the report suggested 'strategies by which future Commonwealth involvement could be made more effective in terms of educational outcomes', in particular outcomes related to 'the attainment by students of satisfactory standards, especially of communication, literacy and numeracy' (Karmel, 1985, p 2). The standards mentioned here were to be achieved by teachers, and the role of government was to ensure the effective allocation of funding for this purpose, which was to be matched to clear objectives and effectiveness indicators specified at the outset through negotiated agreements. A major initiative along these lines was the Australian Government Quality Teacher Program (2000–10), which funded professional development for teachers and school leaders in the period immediately prior to the introduction of NAPLAN, and until it was replaced by national education agreements that drew on the explosion of data afforded by yearly national testing.

This pivot in government policy from inputs to outcomes represented a major shift in logic about how to address inequality. As Egan (2018) has pointed out, for almost the entire period this book covers, the dominant idea underpinning approaches to educational inequalities has been that if disadvantaged children/ young people can succeed in some schools, they should be able to succeed in all, because the key ingredient is teachers and the mechanism for improving achievement is improving their practice.

Drawing on the idea of a 'politics of panic', Mockler (2014) shows how politicians actively stoke public criticism of teachers that contributes to pressure on them to improve. Mockler analysed prime ministerial and ministerial speeches, media releases and interviews, along with related print media articles, produced over a period of one week in September 2012 – the week immediately following the release of the government's response to the Independent Review of School Funding – commonly referred to as the Gonski Review (Gonski et al, 2011). This 'policy moment' was chosen because it represented 'a shift in the public debate on education from issues related to equity and school funding to those related to excellence, quality and school improvement' (Mockler, 2014, p 120). Three 'framing packages' (p 124) emerged from this analysis, the most dominant relating to 'teacher quality' (p 129). Mockler lists the features of this frame as follows: teacher quality is facing a definite crisis that must be addressed; mandated improvements in teaching practices are needed to tackle problems relating to literacy and numeracy; and such practices should reflect a set of technical skills that are measurable and assessable. Within the context of policy focused on outputs and on a technicist understanding of teachers' work, the logic of this framing is self-evident, since teachers bear responsibility for raising achievement standards, no matter what the mitigating circumstances might be.

Consequences: better and fairer?

Perhaps more so than in the case of the policies covered in Chapters 6 and 7, some of the claims about the benefits of prescribing teachers' practice do seem to be borne out by the evidence. There is evidence that policies intended to support the work of teachers have been positively evaluated, such as the English National Literacy Strategy (DfES, 2003), and the Australian Government Quality Teacher Program (Ewing et al, 2004). The latter involved an evaluation of the Action Learning for School Teams project, which was funded by the national government with the aim of promoting quality teaching in a number of priority areas, including literacy, numeracy, and professional standards for teachers and school leaders. What was prescribed in this initiative was teachers' engagement in school-based action learning assisted by an academic partner, which was intended to afford reflection on practice. The reviewers identified a number of factors that contributed to varying degrees of success of the programme and concluded that it has 'been an outstanding success in relation to its central goals of increased professional learning and understanding by school teams' (Ewing et al, 2004, p 92).

Our concern in this chapter is maintaining a balance between supporting teachers' work and prescribing what they do. Getting these kinds of changes right is a fine line, because it depends on a sophisticated understanding of teaching. A commonly described feature of schooling is that classrooms generally operate according to a default mode, or a standard script. It goes something like this: students enter the classroom, sit down and pay attention to the teacher from whom they receive a pedagogical activity; they are expected to respond when questioned; they complete the assigned task individually (or occasionally in groups); on completion they hand in their work or make it available for inspection, before packing up and exiting the room (Johnston and Hayes, 2008). So, it is easy to see how it can be deduced that in getting the teacher bits of these interactions right – that is, behaviour management, lesson structure and pace, activity content and so on – more learning will follow.

This is right up to a point. But teaching is not just about performing or enacting the script, and this is why the same basic script can operate in ways that are engaging and stimulating or in ways that are routine and repetitive. Professor Barbara Comber, a specialist in literacy, details five dimensions of teachers' work related to literacy: interpretive work, pedagogical work, discursive work, relational work and institutional work (Comber, 2006). Hence, teachers' pedagogical work does not occur in isolation. It is set within a broader array of complex and context dependent issues that must also be managed and adjusted to accommodate prescribed pedagogies if they are to be successful. Teaching well requires interpreting and working within the unique context of each school to develop positive and engaging relationships with students and their families, while being accountable to institutional and system demands for accountability, and fine tuning pedagogical practices to meet the needs of each student.

There are few studies that compare the effects of teaching standardisation in schools in poorer and richer areas. When schools in areas of deep disadvantage are included, studies suggest that standardising teaching has the potential to be most damaging. Annette Lareau's (2011) close study of families from middle-class and working-class backgrounds provides some insights into the influence of SES. In more affluent communities, the standard script, which includes ongoing close supervision by adults, is not dissimilar to the cultural norms and expectations that pupils encounter at home. However, in communities where there are high levels of poverty and social exclusion, the standard script affords fewer opportunities for learning and is more difficult to establish and maintain, not only due to the reasons discussed elsewhere and related to more limited resources and narrow curriculum, but also because in these places the routines of schooling, including the ongoing close supervision by adults, are less like the cultural norms and expectations that pupils encounter at home. In these contexts, Lareau (2011) observes that young people are more likely to be independent of adults at an early age since it is not uncommon for them to be required to care for themselves and perhaps younger siblings, and they are justifiably less confident that schooling will work any better for them than their parents and kin before them.

So teachers who are working in already resourced-constrained environments need to adapt their teaching to meet the diverse and deep needs of learners through innovative and sometimes highly differentiated approaches to teaching. The imposition of prescribed pedagogies can tie their hands, especially when combined with a deficit understanding of children and families living in poverty, reflected in a 'pedagogy of poverty' (Haberman, 1991). In classrooms in these contexts, there is a heightened possibility that the substantive purpose of what is being implemented is stripped away, so that what remains is 'a hollowed out form of a more complex textual practice'

Box 8.1: English primary schools: the consequences of prescription and deficit

In the English urban primary schools in which Hempel-Jorgensen and colleagues (2018) explored teachers' conceptualisations of reading, they found that in three of the four schools, teachers' pedagogy was underpinned by an understanding of reading as primarily a matter of proficiency, despite the apparent aim to foster children's desire to read through reading for pleasure (RfP). RfP is a means of disrupting pedagogies of poverty underpinned by deficit understandings of students' abilities linked to their SES. An effect of these approaches is to limit teachers' expectations of what students are capable of achieving. Despite each school's commitment to RfP, a high-profile proficiency agenda was visible in the presence of classroom displays and signs reflecting reading 'ability' hierarchies and a focus on technical aspects of reading. Teachers also used independent reading time to meet the school's assessment or accountability requirements by, for example, marking work, rather than acting as reading role models (Hempel-Jorgensen et al, 2018, p 92). Moreover, children's lack of engaged and sustained reading was not challenged by teachers. It is possible that the teachers had low expectations of these children's engagement as readers and that they were satisfied with them being compliant with the expectation of sitting at their desk with a text. This allowance of minimal engagement with RfP appeared to be at the expense of developing children's intrinsic desire to engage in reading in a more sustained manner (p 93).

(Hayes et al, 2017, p 135), or what Comber and Woods (2016) have described as 'fickle literacies'. 'While there is the surface appearance of working with text and technologies of literacy, many tasks, when closely observed, prove to be practices of compliance – such as copying, cutting and pasting, recitation, and so on' (Comber, 2017, p 59). It is not simply a case of limited rote learning and low-level tasks.

> Unfortunately, these kinds of scripted teaching rituals limit the potential for students to play with appropriate words, to offer alterative meanings, and to connect up their lives to the content of the texts. These missed learning opportunities pass unnoticed but they might have been resources for their writing and speaking. (Hayes et al, 2017, p 178)

When teacher professional development is an exercise in adoption, implementation and evaluation, teachers are required to sharpen their capacity to faithfully implement prescribed pedagogies. The problem is not that teachers are engaged in a process of ongoing evaluation of their practice, but that their professional judgement and assessment of the nature and quality of teaching that should be implemented in their specific local contexts is set aside and replaced by an externally imposed set of practices. Faith in compliance replaces trust in their own professional judgement and in their ability to discern how best to support their pupils' learning needs.

> **Box 8.2: Northern primary schools: compliance dislodging professional capability**
>
> In the case of Northern primary schools (Hayes et al, 2017), when the research was conducted, all primary schools in South Australia were required to develop agreements about how to improve literacy from Reception to Year 7. These comprehensive agreements included information about the scope and sequence for teaching literacy, the form and timing of assessment tasks, and a comprehensive set of information intended to support a whole-school approach to improving students' performance in literacy. The local nature of these agreements was intended to strengthen the likelihood that the approaches to literacy they contained were supported by teachers committed to their adoption. The Northern primary schools' teachers received relevant specialist training, and student progress was regularly assessed. Despite these coordinated local efforts, the literacy levels of pupils in the three schools remained persistently low, before and over the duration of the study. The majority of teachers made efforts to implement the intended practices faithfully. Their classrooms were well organised, the students were kept busy on set tasks, and the lessons proceeded with minimal disruption. However, the implementation of 'what works' tended to prioritise compliance over teacher judgement. Even some very experienced teachers ceded their authority to an authorised approach to literacy learning.

So the problems described in Chapters 3, 4, and 5, such as narrower curriculum and less stimulating lessons, and children learning less, becoming demotivated and feeling that they do not belong in school, are not just problems caused by testing regimes and excessive accountability. In misunderstanding processes of learning and teaching, particularly the nature of teachers' work, policy makers have underestimated the value and potential of teachers, when properly resourced, to support students' learning. They have limited the difference that teachers can make, especially in the areas where it matters most.

9

Mistake #4: misunderstanding educational inequalities

The fourth mistake that we identify is a failure to understand the causes of educational inequalities.

As described in Chapter 2, the period covered by this book has been one in which, although living standards overall have risen, inequalities have widened, labour market insecurity has increased, economic opportunities have narrowed in certain 'left-behind' places, and global conflicts and disasters have brought new disadvantaged populations to under-resourced urban neighbourhoods. In these circumstances, educational inequalities would be expected to widen.

Policies to create more equitable systems have featured prominently at some points in English and Australian policy history. But the approaches taken have been inconsistent and sometimes contradictory. Mostly what has been done has been insufficient, sometimes misdirected or counterproductive. In this chapter, we describe what has been done and why, and explain why overall it has failed to achieve the desired result.

Policies to tackle educational inequalities

In England, policies to address inequalities have a long history but have taken very different forms. One distinctive strand, favoured by Labour governments, has been top-up programmes and funds directed at disadvantaged places and/or groups. These started in the 1960s with Educational Priority Areas (EPAs) and additional funding to support education for EAL pupils. They were substantially increased during the Labour government's

13 years in power from 1997, with Education Action Zones (EAZs), Excellence in Cities (EiC) and City Challenges, as well as additional grants for interventions such as learning mentors and reading catch-up. In 2002, Teach First was established to attract high-achieving graduates into teaching in disadvantaged schools (see Lupton and Obolenskaya [2013] for a fuller review). However, this Labour government also deployed mainstream policies to target the most challenging areas and close gaps. As described in Chapters 6, 7 and 8, Labour's academies programme, replacing 'failing' schools in 'deprived' areas, was explicitly badged as an attempt to even up school quality, as was its National Challenge initiative and its use of floor targets and inspection. Standardisation of teaching was also motivated by making sure that children received the same input wherever they lived. Under Labour 1997–2010, redistribution of mainstream funding also became a major tool. Revenue funding for schools was increasingly bent towards those dealing with greater need, as was a new programme of school rebuilding: Building Schools for the Future. There were major funding programmes such as the Education Maintenance Allowance to support students to stay on in education after the age of 16. And towards the latter part of Labour's term in office, there were moves to rebalance the content of curriculum in the interests of greater inclusion and equity. From 2005, Labour allowed vocational awards to count as equivalent to GCSEs in school performance tables, aiming to recognise a wider range of achievement and promote broader engagement. From 2007, a wider outcomes framework was established (Every Child Matters), with 'enjoy and achieve' being just one of five dimensions with which all organisations dealing with children should be concerned. The others were health, safety, economic well-being and making a positive contribution.

The Conservative–Liberal Democrat coalition government elected in 2010 eschewed the policy of targeted grants and programmes, abolishing most of them. The idea of targeting particular places with low educational achievement only re-emerged in 2017 in a small scale way with the launch of 12 Opportunity Areas – this time mainly in smaller industrial towns or coastal areas. Instead, it introduced the

Pupil Premium (PP), a new individually targeted funding scheme. PP is a per capita grant to be spent in whichever way schools choose to raise the achievement of pupils identified as disadvantaged. Different in approach, it has nevertheless resulted in further redistribution to schools with the least advantaged intakes (Lupton and Thomson, 2015). As noted in Chapter 7, increasingly sophisticated measures for monitoring disadvantage gaps and holding autonomous schools to account has also been a feature of the coalition (and later Conservative) approach. But the coalition/Conservatives took a very different approach to curriculum: reversing Labour's decision to count vocational equivalents; introducing the English Baccalaureate (a combination of traditional academic subjects) as a core in secondary schools; and revising curriculum content in subjects like English and history to comprise more traditional content (Lupton and Thomson, 2015; Lupton and Obolenskaya, 2020).

Australia also has a long history of efforts to equalise educational inputs and outcomes. In 1972, the Whitlam government was elected with an education reform mandate and money was directed towards making schooling fairer through the creation of the Disadvantaged Schools Program that spanned the period 1973–96. The initiative was an effort to coordinate at the national level the provision of additional resources to schools serving communities experiencing high levels of marginalisation and poverty, although by no means all 'disadvantaged schools' met the funding criteria. During that period, and subsequently, there have also been separate arrangements to support the schooling experiences of students from a range of equity groups. These were initially coordinated by the Schools Commission until it was abolished in 1987 but not before it developed the National Policy for the Education of Girls in Australia (1987) – the first national policy in the area of schooling. Subsequently, joint decisions on shared priorities and agreed national initiatives have been made through intergovernmental policy councils. These include 'top-up' programmes for the states and territories, and since 2009, formal agreements between the Australian government and state and territory educational authorities – including public, private and Catholic systems. Initially, these formal agreements targeted improving teacher quality, literacy and numeracy, as well as the schooling experiences of young people in settings where there are high levels of disadvantage. Since the start of 2019, these have been replaced by National School Reform Agreements that target eight reforms, including: enhancing the Australian curriculum to support teacher assessment of student attainment and growth; providing opt-in online learning assessment tools to assist teachers; strengthening the initial teacher education accreditation system; introducing a national USI; and an independent national evidence institute to inform teacher practice, system improvement and policy development. While the National School Reform Agreements set targets for improving the academic achievement of all students, including priority equity cohorts, the eight national reforms that have been identified do not specifically support these targets.

However, a key difference between the two countries is in the distribution of mainstream funding. As explained in Chapter 6, needs-based funding was a key principle of the Whitlam government, and a motivator for the extension of state aid to non-government schools. However, this lasted just long enough to address the most serious resourcing deficiencies in inner-city government and Catholic schools. Subsequent governments, beginning with that of Malcolm Fraser in 1975, gradually moved towards entrenching choice as the dominant funding logic. While federal and state funds are distributed to some extent according to recognised need, these arrangements benefit and over-invest in schools with more advantaged intakes (Bonnor and Shepherd, 2017). The bias in federal funding towards non-government schools has increased dramatically since the Howard government (1996–2007), and by the 2016–17 financial year, the Commonwealth's contribution per FTE student was $2,645 for students enrolled in government schools, and $8,053 for students enrolled in non-government schools. The reports of David Gonski (Gonski et al, 2011, 2018), which argued for a needs-based funding approach, are the closest Australia has come to correcting what Adam Rorris, the education economist who managed the school resourcing taskforce between 2002 and 2008, has described as a 'grotesque policy disaster' (Baker, 2019).

Policy rationales

Policies on educational inequalities have taken such different forms at different times partly because governments have had different views on the best means to achieve their ends – whether to target areas or individuals, for example. But they have also served different political objectives. Pursued by governments of Right and Left, they have aimed sometimes at 'social justice' or 'equity', sometimes at 'equality of opportunity' or 'equality of outcomes' or 'social mobility', and these goals themselves have been held in tension with others, such as parental choice.

One consistent rationale, perhaps particularly in England, has been 'levelling up' – ensuring *equal* standards of provision everywhere. This is evident in a whole range of programmes: capital spending to improve school buildings; schemes to incentivise teacher recruitment and retention; target setting and inspection; and policies to support, or takeover/academise, 'failing' schools in poorer areas. It has also been behind efforts to raise the quality of teaching and leadership as described in Chapter 8.

However, levelling up through funding redistribution is politically contested. As shown in Chapter 6, competition between schools driven by consumer choice can also be seen as a way of levelling up quality, instead of what might be perceived as government bail-outs or state interventions to equalise intakes. Parental choice itself may also be valued as a competing principle with equity, as has been the case for long periods in Australian history, making it electorally risky to shift the balance more towards needs-based allocations. As Windle puts it:

> The market model provides a permanent buffer for government from blame about the quality of the school system as a whole.... The promise of choice means that there are no serious attempts to redress the social segregation of student populations, even though this appears to be one of the most powerful levers to reducing inequality. (Windle, 2014, p 320)

In the same vein, school and teacher improvement is a less controversial strategy for governments than targeting disadvantaged pupils specifically, because it holds the appeal of improvements for *all* children (Mockler, 2014).

Another prominent, but contested, policy rationale is that education should be substantively different for poorer/richer students or in poorer/richer places. In one sense, it is widely accepted that schools in disadvantaged areas are likely to need to dismantle 'barriers' to learning arising from poverty, such as hunger or lack of access to books at home, or to work experience. These issues have been tackled by funding for individuals (for example, through PP, which might buy a uniform, or pay for trips or additional tutoring and mentoring) or for schools or areas (for example, to enable schools to run breakfast clubs or employ family support workers). However, whether the substance of education (curriculum and pedagogy) needs to be different in different circumstances has been hotly contested, resulting in significant swings in policy approach. Contextualised approaches to curriculum and pedagogy are at the heart of many progressive approaches around the world. Educators in this tradition have argued that equitable educational experiences only occur when curriculum content reflects learners' own experiences and identities and when teaching is empowering, enabling voice, choice and control (Connell, 1992, 2012). Schools may also need to do different things to support and engage families. These approaches have been more a feature of Australian than English policy, particularly through the Disadvantaged Schools Program (DSP). However, as Thomson (2007) describes, DSP became, over time, more centrally framed and focused on attainment outcomes, in contrast to its earlier progressive socially oriented approach. And in both countries, as discussed in Chapter 8, contextualised approaches to curriculum and pedagogy have been 'trumped' for some time by standardised approaches and an emphasis on embedding practices that 'work'.

Since 2010 in England, the Conservatives' curriculum reforms, heavily influenced by the work of E.D. Hirsch, have reflected the idea that giving everyone access to the same 'core knowledge' is a better foundation for greater equality than differentiating what is learned. As schools minister Nick Gibb (2015a, pp 15–16) put it, 'our reforms were based on a desire to see social justice through equalising the unfair distribution of intellectual capital in British society'. 'The body of academic knowledge', he argued, 'belongs to everyone, regardless of background, circumstance or job' (p 16). Everyone is entitled to have the chance to learn it, rather than having a curriculum designed to develop understanding and skills and/or one that follows children's own enquiries but may deprive them of the opportunity to gain 'powerful knowledge', different from that which they could gain outside school (Young, 2013). Some English academies, including our case study school Dreamfields (Kulz, 2017), have also been influenced by evidence from US Charter Schools, which have been successful in raising academic achievement by extending learning hours and establishing strict disciplinary codes to compensate for perceived lack of structure and discipline at home and to divert/isolate young people from neighbourhood risks.

Consequences: better and fairer?

We do not claim that all of the policies pursued in this period have been unsuccessful. Evaluated individually and in their own terms, some have shown positive results. It is also the case that some aspects of inequality have lessened. More working-class students are going to higher education; girls and some minority ethnic groups have made substantial progress (see Francis et al, 2017c). However, taking the broad and long view (see Chapter 1), it is abundantly clear that, in sum, the policies followed have not created a situation of educational equity, social justice, equality of opportunity, social mobility or however such objectives might be framed. This is so transparently true that, in contrast to our approach in Chapters 6, 7 and 8, we spend less time in this chapter examining detailed evidence of specific policy successes and failures and more time exploring why decades of policy have made so little difference. Reviewing the extensive literature on this topic leads us to four main reasons.

The first is that policy makers have been 'looking in the wrong place' (Ball, 2017, p 168) for policies that could really reduce educational inequalities. Success in education is not just a product of the quality of schooling but of multiple 'social determinants' – family income and wealth; physical and mental health; housing and neighbourhood conditions and so on – just as good health is not solely a product of the quality of health services. This has been abundantly evident during the COVID-19 pandemic, which has triggered mainstream political concern about learning gaps for disadvantaged and vulnerable children, who are, for example, less likely than their better-off peers to complete work at home and less likely to be able to manage without the free meals, support and other services that schools provide. But this should not have been a surprise. For decades, studies of 'school effects' have shown that about 10 to 20 per cent of differences in educational outcomes are down to schools, the rest being down to individual, household and neighbourhood factors (Kerr and West, 2010). And when social policy researchers Kerris Cooper and Kitty Stewart of the London School of Economics and Political Science conducted a systematic review of international studies of the relationships between family income and educational outcomes, they found clear evidence of a causal relationship between poverty and worse outcomes. Their estimates suggest that increasing the income of families eligible for FSM in England to the average for non-FSM families could halve the attainment gap at KS2, even if nothing different were done in schools (Cooper and Stewart, 2013, 2017). This being the case, the evidence that PP funding in England has made very little impact on attainment gaps is entirely to be expected, given that it came at a time of stringent cuts to the incomes of low-income families through the tax and benefits system.

Another aspect of 'looking in the wrong place' has been an increasing tendency to understand educational inequality as a problem experienced by individuals, rather than by groups of people. This is reflected in the identification of individual 'barriers' to learning, shifting the focus away from how to make school practices as a whole more equitable, and sometimes in 'deficit' explanations that locate the problem with families who are said to lack what it takes to enable educational success – usually aspiration, engagement, structure and discipline. It is perhaps understandable that individual teachers focus on individuals and families, since that is who they deal with. But

Box 9.1: Parkside Academy: taking young people's lives into account

Salokangas and Ainscow's (2018) study of Parkside Academy gives an insight into the multiple 'social determinants' of educational experiences and outcomes confronting young people in an inner-urban area. It is important to acknowledge and understand the life circumstances of these young people, so that schooling practices afford them opportunities rather than further barriers to be overcome. The majority of students came from low-income families. The unemployment rate in the area was more than four times as high as the national average and for some young people in particular, employment prospects seemed particularly bleak. Eighty per cent of Black youths in the area were unemployed, according to local data. Many students at the school were from homeless families, due to a concentration of homeless family housing units in the neighbourhood, and some were from Traveller families, and had experienced intermittent schooling careers. There were high levels of family fracture. About half the school's intake were living in one-parent families or with family members other than parents, or in foster homes, and one result of this was that many acted as carers for siblings or other family members. Many of the students were new arrivals to the country, speaking or writing little or no English. Some had limited previous experiences of formal education on arrival. Most lived in the Green End neighbourhood, which was notorious for race riots in the 1980s and had more contemporary problems with high levels of gang-related and gun crimes. Living in Green End was risky for young people and meant that they also carried with them the stigmatised reputation of the area.

policies that rest on the transformation of individual failings are bound to have only limited effects, because they miss the bigger causes of the problem. As Wrigley (2018) points out in a discussion of the north-east of England, what is holding young people's life chances back is not their individual aspirations but the lack of replacement employment after the collapse of shipyards and steelworks. Whether derived from what social policy academic Professor Ruth Levitas (2005) described as a 'moral underclass discourse' or from a 'social integrationist discourse', which emphasises reconnecting people who have become marginalised, the transference of responsibility to individuals shifts attention from systemic inequalities such as racism, unequal economic opportunities and accumulated differences in wealth.

This does not mean that individual schools or individual teachers cannot make a difference or that individual young people cannot succeed against the odds. They can and they do. But the flip side of expecting teachers and schools to transform educational outcomes in the absence of wider action is that attention is shifted away from bigger societal problems onto the actions of schools. Equity becomes narrowly conceived as a problem of quality. It is left to 'heroic' educational leaders and teachers to shoulder the responsibility for ensuring fairness and quality (Thrupp, 1999; Loughland and Thompson, 2016, p 127).

With that in mind, it seems clear that the second reason that education policies have failed to make a difference is that the scale of funding redistribution has been insufficient. Redistributing funding according to need is the right thing to do. Evidence from robust economic studies clearly demonstrates that resources make a difference (McNally, 2015). This is not just because barriers faced by individuals should be dismantled by additional support and intervention, but also because dealing with concentrated poverty and disadvantage creates extra workload and pressures for schools, such as catering for a very diverse range of needs and languages; chasing up attendance; engaging parents who have low expectations of education; managing raised emotions; liaising with other organisations; and so on.

In Australia, there is a clear problem with lack of needs-based funding. Young people attending schools in disadvantaged communities continue to miss out as government schools where disadvantage is disproportionately concentrated are significantly less well funded than similar schools in other sectors, both in terms of public and private funding (Thompson et al, 2019). Kenway describes Australian schooling as 'layers of disadvantage and advantage across all sectors' (2013, p 286). But even in England, where funding in the state system is redistributive, the costs of educating a student in the most disadvantaged school in the country is a fraction of the fees for elite public schools, and a fraction of the public and private money that is put in to educate the average middle-class child. To really tackle inequalities, educational resources would need to be significantly greater in poorer areas on the grounds that children

> ## Box 9.2: Waterwell Primary School: the burden of securing a fair test for all students
>
> At Waterwell Primary School, Comber (2012) observed that 'it takes more work and time to successfully manage standardised testing in such schools than it does in schools where the student population is largely Anglo and middle-class' (p 126). Teachers reported that this was partly because children from more disadvantaged homes and/or whose first language was not English needed them to 'warm them up' to the format, such as prompts and clues in the test, 'because you know, they can miss that bubble over there which says *colour two boxes*, you know, if you only colour one you're going to get it wrong' (teacher, cited in Comber, 2012, p 128 emphasis in original). It was also partly because of the administrative and relational aspects of managing the tests, such as negotiating student withdrawal, since children can be withdrawn if they are new arrivals to Australia and learning English. Gaining parent/caregiver signatures and explaining results to parents and children were more 'complex and resource intensive when families do not speak, read or write English' (p 127). Comber notes that 'the extra work compounds exponentially in low-socioeconomic contexts and it occurs at the expense of other activities' (p 127).

with the least advantages at home both need and deserve the best teachers, buildings, resources and opportunities that the system can offer. There have been glimpses of such approaches: Labour's Building Schools for the Future initiative, the DSP, and the Teach First and Teach for Australia programmes (if one accepts that high-flying graduates with limited training are 'better' than experienced teachers). But in general, the position that poorer people should get *better* schools can be politically difficult for governments to maintain. Extra resources are more commonly directed through temporary or spatially limited top-up programmes rather than shifts in mainstream funding allocations.

Third, policies on educational inequalities have focused too much on educational attainment – a result of the focus on markets and on numbers described in Chapters 6 and 7. Attainment is important. But the shift from a 'social democratic' conceptualisation of equity to a market conceptualisation (Rizvi, 2013) risks leaving out a lot of other elements of education fairness, such as whether people have equal opportunities to pursue the things that are important to them, and whether they are treated equally, and their cultures and identities recognised to the same extent (Fraser, 1997; Gewirtz, 1998; Raffo, 2014). This is not just a philosophical point. As we have demonstrated throughout this book, when school practices are aimed too much at raising academic standards and disregard other aspects of educational equity, they can end up creating new disparities and injustices. When such a lot of school activity is geared to the importance of performance on a selected few items of knowledge and competence, children struggle to define themselves other than in these terms. Opportunities to be recognised, celebrated and valued for personal qualities and achievements in other arenas become more limited. These limitations play into the hands of families who once again are not only better positioned in the race for academic qualifications but can provide wider opportunities for their children through private means. Participants in Neumann and colleagues' (2020) study reported that contrary to the 'Hirschian ideal' that 'hard knowledge' would offer access to cultural capital and mitigate social inequalities, the 'one-size-fits-all' new curriculum and performance pressures demotivated disadvantaged students and those with additional needs and made it more difficult for them to succeed. Moreover, pressures on raising attainment in the short term can be a disincentive for schools to work in long-term ways with other agencies to support children, families and communities (Crowther et al, 2003). Tilting the balance exclusively towards attainment can mean schools can end up being part of the problem as well as part of the solution.

Finally and perhaps most fundamentally, policies have failed because they have insufficiently addressed the point that inequality is double-sided, affected not just by the conditions and behaviours of the poor but those of the rich. Education is not only (or mainly) valuable to individuals for itself but because it confers advantage in the competition for jobs, income and status. So families with financial, social and/or intellectual resources invest them in education to give their children a head start. The most obvious example is paying for private schooling. But advantage and privilege are sought in myriad ways: paying for out-of-school experiences and hobbies; investing in books, educational toys and software; moving to the catchment area of a good school; and using networks of family, friends and professional associates to research and secure work experience or university places. In England in 2019, 27 per cent of 11–16-year-olds had received private tuition, rising to 41 per cent in London (The Sutton Trust, 2019), indicating that topping up free education in state schools is not just the preserve of a rich minority but a symptom of an escalating 'arms race' for credentials and secure futures (Weale, 2018). These behaviours necessarily confer disadvantage on those who cannot afford them, just as the competitive behaviour of schools that 'cream-skim' students disadvantages neighbouring schools, which are left with dwindling enrolments and disproportionately high needs. Education policies can reduce educational inequalities, but they can also increase them.

This means that governments that are really committed to greater equity or equality in education should not only heavily overcompensate through additional funding and opportunities, but also scrutinise the effects of their other education (and social) policies. In both England and Australia, there have been periods of education policy where this has been recognised. But consistently this has not been the case. On the whole, too much has been expected of education policies, while other social policies have worked in the opposite direction, redistribution has been insufficient and 'equal outcomes' have been defined too narrowly. And the problem has been blamed either on poor children and families or on school leaders and teachers, obscuring the real issues and leaving policy makers without the tools to actually do anything about it. Meanwhile education policies that create inequalities have been actively pursued, including expanding markets, funding and supporting private and selective schools, promoting competition and differentiation, and incentivising exclusion.

Ball writes in his book *The Education Debate* (2017) that the different ways in which wider inequalities affect education, and the ways in which education itself creates inequalities while at the same time offering potential to ameliorate them, seem 'thoroughly confused within policy' (p 210). We agree. Given that, it is not surprising that, overall, little impact has been made on the problem.

10

Mistake #5: leaving education out of education policy making

Our fifth mistake relates to the nature of education policy making and the characteristics of policy processes.

Our central argument is that for a variety of reasons and in a variety of ways, educational policy making has become increasingly divorced from knowledge of educational theory and practice. This is not to say that the knowledge of teachers, school leaders, academics and researchers who study teaching, learning and other aspects of the educational day-to-day is the *only* kind of knowledge that should count in education policy. As with many of the issues we have discussed, the problem is not that everything that has happened is bad, but that the balance has tipped too far in one direction, making it more likely that the wrong decisions will be made and that established policies will continue to be followed even when the evidence is clear that they are mistaken.

In this chapter, we draw on research about policy, rather than about specific policies as we have done in earlier chapters. We describe some of the problems with education policy-making processes in England and Australia, how they have come about, and why we think they are getting in the way of making education better and fairer.

Long-standing problems in education policy making

In their book on social policy mistakes in England, King and Crewe (2014) identify 12 factors that lead to 'policy blunders'. Five of these come under the category of 'human errors':

cultural disconnect (policy makers not understanding that other people's lives are not like their own); group-think; prejudice and pragmatism; operational disconnect (policy makers not understanding how policies will play out on the ground); and panic, symbols and spin. The others are 'system failures': the independence of Whitehall departments; the rapid turnover of ministers and civil servants; the increasingly activist role of ministers; lack of ministerial accountability (particularly for the long-term consequences of their actions); the weak role of parliament in the English system; asymmetries of expertise especially with private sector partners; and a deficit of deliberation in the making of policy. System failures make human errors more likely and more damaging.

Education policy research points to education being particularly prone to some of these human errors, not least the commonly recognised problem of ministers relying on their own knowledge of schooling and their own prejudices. Recall, for example, the insistence of English Prime Minister Theresa May (herself a pupil at a grammar school that became a comprehensive) that expanding grammar schools would increase social mobility (Whittaker, 2016), despite a barrage of research evidence showing the opposite (Andrews et al, 2016; Gorard and Siddiqui, 2018). Cultural disconnect is starkly in evidence in England's return to a traditional curriculum, as illustrated in Chapter 4. The manufacturing of crises is a recurrent problem in both countries (Mockler, 2014), prompted at four-year intervals by PISA 'shocks'.

Of more interest in the context of this book are 'system failures', since these are perhaps more susceptible to beneficial reform. Previous chapters of this book bring some persistent system failures sharply into view. One of these, as discussed in Chapter 9, is the separation of education from other social policies, such that teachers are expected to transform educational outcomes while other social policies work in opposite directions. Another, underpinning most of the problems we describe, and a prime motivator for us in writing this book, is the lack of constructive deliberation. Contests between competing versions of what education should deliver and for whom, and who should control it, are long-standing in educational policy. They have been particularly bitter in recent years – with the expertise of teachers, school leaders and researchers often deliberately dismissed as being too wedded to past ideas or beliefs, blocking progress, and ideological rather than evidential – but they are not new.

So we do not 'hark back' to a golden age of consensus in which education and social policies were seamlessly integrated. But we do argue that a series of interconnected changes in the period covered by this book has exacerbated some existing system failures and increased the likelihood of human errors. In particular, educational policy making has become increasingly separated from educational knowledge.

Changes in education policy-making processes

Education policy research points to four main changes in recent decades. One is the globalisation of policy. Ball explains that globalisation has produced 'a set of imperatives for policy at the national level and a particular way of thinking about education and its contemporary problems and purposes' – that is, the focus on maximising human capital for economic competitiveness (Ball, 2017, p 31). More than that, it has created a new 'spatial frame' for policy making, with policies no longer made entirely within nation states but as a result of international policy flows. Countries look to each other and the OECD to identify successful policy approaches, and are influenced by global firms (edu-businesses and consultancies such as Pearson and McKinsey) and philanthropies (such as Teach for All).

What emerges is not exactly replicated policies, since borrowed policies must necessarily fit to existing national systems. Rather, what we see is a 'paradigm convergence', or as Ball describes it:

> [t]he invocation of policies with common underlying principles, similar operational mechanisms and similar first order effects and second order effects: first order effects in terms of their impact on practitioners, practice and institutional procedures and second order effects in terms of social justice – patterns of access, opportunity and outcome. (Ball, 1999, p 198)

Ball has also described a 'generic global policy ensemble' (2017, p 61), characterised by market forms, the technologies of NPM and cultures of performativity marshalled through data monitoring, and inspection. Finnish policy maker Pasi Sahlberg (2012, 2015), has described a Global Education Reform Movement (GERM) characterised by standardised teaching and learning, a focus on literacy and numeracy, teaching a prescribed curriculum, market-oriented reforms, and test-based accountability and control – the mistakes described in Chapters 6, 7 and 8.

A second important change is upscaling of decision making within countries – sometimes described as centralisation. As noted in Chapters 2 and 7, England's already Westminster-dominated system and Australia's federal system have become increasingly centralised over time: in Australia mainly in the past decade or so since the introduction of NAPLAN and in England since the ERA 1988, although increasing since 2010 with the declining role of LEAs in running schools and allocating school funding. One element of this is a shift in power from the local state to the national state, resulting in what is described in the Australian literature as 'ministerialisation'. Yates and colleagues (2011, p 519) argue that the increasing interest shown by the federal government in education since it started funding schools in the 1960s has moved control of the curriculum away from education departments of the public service, so that it is now 'directly the purview of Ministers and for which they are to be held accountable'. Ministers, by their own admission, do not necessarily know anything about education, which has (in English schools minister Nick Gibb's words) 'developed a language of its own, erecting barriers to entry for the interested layman' (Gibb, 2015a, p 13). Gibb admitted he 'needed a crash course in education theory and debates' when he became Shadow Minister for Education (Gibb, 2015a, p 18).

This system change clearly increases the risk of individual policy errors arising from cultural disconnect or prejudice as well as bringing educational decisions into short-term political cycles in which ministers need to demonstrate impact. At the same time, decisions that were formerly matters for practitioners (such as schemes of work and the structure of lessons) have become matters of policy. 'Teacher autonomy' is frequently held up as something politicians want to encourage, but as described in Chapter 8, less and less of what teachers do is actually determined by teachers. The shift to centralised policy making also cuts out practising educators in another way. It brings policy decisions into a smaller bubble of influence – ministers, civil servants, selected advisers, leaders of national organisations and capital city-based think tanks – whereas locally based decision making tends to involve greater involvement of those close to the ground. Ball (2017, p 125) suggests that in the English context, 'sources of innovation and fresh thinking from outside London have been cut off'. In Australia, Loughland and Thompson (2016) point out that the imperative for think tanks to produce media friendly and politically expedient reports tends to sideline context, complexity and nuance.

A third trend has been expansion and change in the range of actors and influencers involved in policy-making processes including 'policy knowing' – the production of knowledge that informs policy making. Although the formal power in policy making has been centralised, policy space has simultaneously become 'more dispersed' and more 'crowded' (Ball, 2017, p 220), with multiple new actors such as academy chains, charities (for example, EEF and Teach First), edu-businesses, philanthropists, think tanks, and individual thought leaders and consultants including prominent teachers and head teachers (Gunter et al, 2015). These organisations and individuals compete for influence but also collaborate formally and informally in what Ball and Junemann (2012) have described as new networks of education governance.

At the same time, ways of 'policy knowing' have also changed, as technology has opened access to knowledge and enabled multiple new voices to be heard, without the structure and filters of a formal 'curriculum' managed by gatekeepers such as academics, peer-reviewed journals, government departments and established research institutes. Large volumes of information can be found very quickly, and knowledge may also be generated very quickly – through tweets, blogs and webinars – and discarded very quickly. New 'knowledge brokers' such as charities and teacher organisations have emerged to manage, package and disseminate bite-sized knowledge chunks (Moss, 2016). Universities and academic researchers have tended to become less influential as the education policy space has become more crowded, even regardless of any marginalisation on ideological grounds and the climate of increasing suspicion of 'experts' (Edwards and Potts, 2008, p 124). In contrast to some of the new 'knowers', they devote fewer resources to communications and influencing, work on longer timescales and publish behind academic journal paywalls (Lupton and Hayes, 2018). In both Australia and England, the increasing prescription of teacher education, and in England its dispersal to schools and trusts, has further weakened the visibility of academic research to education practitioners.

Fourth and linked to this trend, there have been changes in the types of evidence used to inform education policy decisions. Associated with the boom in quantitative data, quantitative research has become much more common and more influential. One especially noticeable trend has been the growth of the discipline of economics of education, associated with increasing policy interest in human capital and 'returns' to educational qualifications, and with the efficiency and effectiveness of education systems. A more recent development, accelerating over the past decade, is the movement towards evidence-based policy and practice, or the 'what works' approach described in Chapter 8. While not limited to education (the UK government funds 'what works centres' in a number of policy areas), 'what works' has had a particular appeal in education, coming after multiple critiques of the field of educational research for not providing enough clear evidence of what schools and teachers should actually do (Tooley and Darby, 1998; Bennett, 2013; Goldacre, 2013). It relies on three steps:

- the identification of successful or unsuccessful practices through randomised controlled trials or quasi-experimental studies – studies comparing groups receiving an educational intervention and those not;
- systematic review (meta-analysis) of multiple studies of the same kinds of intervention;

- review of reviews (meta-meta-analysis) to compare the relative effectiveness of different kinds of intervention (for example, setting homework versus use of teaching assistants).

In England, this kind of evidence (synthesised by EEF) is not only vigorously promoted to schools by DfE as described in Chapter 8. It also sits at the top of a formal hierarchy of evidence used in assessing school funding bids, thus further influencing the kind of knowledge that is valued and used in practice. 'Expert opinion/advice' from consultants and academics sits close to the bottom, just above 'media stories' and 'anecdote' (DfE, 2017). Beyond EEF, other sources of knowledge of 'what works' are globally influential, in particular the meta-analytic work of Melbourne-based Professor John Hattie – famously described by the *Times Education Supplement* as the search for teaching's 'Holy Grail'. Hattie's *Visible Learning* (2009) synthesised 800 meta-analyses (50,000 individual studies) in order to rank different influences on learning by their 'effect sizes'.

Consequences

These changes in policy-making processes cannot be seen simplistically as the *cause* of the mistaken policies described in Chapters 6 to 9. For one thing, in most cases the original mistakes – marketising school systems, introducing standardised tests and so on – occurred before or simultaneously with these changes. The ways in which policy making has changed are in some respects *symptoms* of the same conditions and logics that produced those policy decisions: global economic competition; global flows of people and ideas; and the political dominance of market liberalism and social conservatism over social democratic, egalitarian and progressive modes of thought and opinion. Reliance on economic research and evidence of 'what works' to produce optimum test outcomes arises because we have come to think of education as an economic 'production function' in which spending produces inputs, outputs and ultimately economic outcomes in the form of knowledge, skills, earnings, productivity and growth. In other respects, the changes in policy making are themselves accumulated products of major policy decisions. For instance, one reason that a wider range of actors has become involved in education policy making is that the marketisation of education systems has created new stakeholders with interests in the outcomes of policy. However, it is also the case that the ways in which policies are currently made, including their evidential bases, omissions and exclusions, create new kinds of 'path dependencies'. They make it less likely that existing ways of doing things can be challenged and changed, and more likely that new mistakes will be made, reinforcing the old.

One major unintended consequence is that evidence is often misunderstood, and thus misused in regimes of monitoring and target setting and in guidance to teachers and leaders. The meaning of test results is a particular problem. Educational tests have different purposes and are designed accordingly. Some are designed to check whether everyone has reached an absolute level of knowledge or skills. Others are designed to enable students across a range of ability to demonstrate what they can do, so test items are written so that about 50% of students get them right. These purposes are not always distinguished in the setting of political objectives or in claims about the effects of policies. Sometimes grade boundaries in full-cohort tests are set relative to absolute levels. Sometimes they are set relative to norms, meaning that roughly the same proportion will achieve each grade regardless of whether the 'standard' has gone up or down. Tests usually have high levels of measurement error and interpretation difficulties are exacerbated when there are small samples (Wu, 2010, 2016). A particular problem is that assessing the adequacy of students' progress over time, between one test and another, is difficult, not only because of measurement error in the point-in-time tests, but because trajectories of learning are genuinely very variable. In England, social statistics experts Professors George Leckie and Harvey Goldstein (2017) have demonstrated how the new Progress 8 measure designed to hold schools to account penalises those with more disadvantaged intakes because, as well as having lower starting points, such students typically make less progress. Meanwhile the Education Datalab's (2016) analysis challenges the whole idea of setting progress targets and dividing students into progression pathways.

It shows that most children make either more progress or less progress than the expected amount used to set targets for individuals and schools, and progress is not linear. Predictions are inaccurate for most children, and particularly poor for those with lower attainment at the start. Unless these nuances of the meaning of test results are understood, policies for teaching and learning and expectations of teachers and schools will be misdirected, and they are.

Another example is evidence from 'what works' studies – the 'effect sizes' that underpin the toolkits and rankings being sold to teachers and school leaders to help them decide which practices will be most effective, and which ready-made packages and programmes to buy from commercial suppliers and consultants. These have a ready simplicity – interventions with the largest effect sizes are the ones that are most effective. But unfortunately that is not necessarily true either. The reasons are explained by Durham University mathematics education specialist Professor Adrian Simpson, who works through the technical problems in detail, drawing on close knowledge of multiple studies (Simpson, 2017, 2018). Simpson explains that although the 'effect size' calculation appears simple, there 'are considerable subtleties in understanding it sufficiently well to ensure that the processes of combining effect sizes in meta-analyses allows valid conclusions to be drawn' (Simpson, 2017, p 452). Effect sizes are not, as they are purported to be, measures of the effectiveness of the intervention, but of the sensitivity of the research design – the nature of the intervention, the test of outcomes, and the 'treatment' and 'control or comparison' groups. Studies that compare outcomes on standardised tests, for example, have been shown to have much smaller effect sizes than ones that use researcher-designed tests that specifically test a narrower range of things covered in the intervention. So when we see an effect size reported for an intervention (for example, that it improves learning by x months) we need to know the detail of what was done, who participated, what and who this was compared with, and the details of the measured outcome. So, as Simpson puts it (pp 453–4), 'one cannot generally compare across studies, and one cannot reasonably combine studies to obtain an estimate of the impact of a class of interventions'. Taking the same example used earlier in the chapter, it is meaningless to compare 'homework' and 'teaching assistants' on the basis of averaged effect sizes from multiple studies. Used simplistically, there is a grave danger that policy and practice will be misdirected. Simpson again: 'These meta-meta-analyses which order areas on the basis of effect size are ... poor selection mechanisms for driving educational policy and should not be used for directing large portions of a country's education budget' (Simpson, 2017, pp 455–6).

These errors of understanding, in the context of pressures to raise 'standards' as measured by test results, have critical consequences for children and young people. Unrealistically high or low achievement targets are set; lessons are governed by adherence to standardised practices and programmes that are deemed to 'work'; school reputations are damaged, leaving it hard for them to recruit and retain teachers or maintain their enrolments and funding; and schools are closed.

At the same time, valuable knowledge is disregarded. Focusing on the 'hard evidence' of test results, international surveys and 'what works' studies provides policy makers with answers they cannot get from smaller scale studies of practice – answers to questions such as 'would it be more productive to invest in this approach or that one?' But it also implies particular understandings of the problem and the solution: a focus on individual and classroom intervention rather than system or structural responses; theories of learning as a linear developmental process; and theories of knowledge as a set of causal relationships verifiable through experiments. Combined with the upscaling of policy making and the change in personnel involved in policy-making processes, reliance on this kind of evidence creates a situation in which knowledge of educational theory and practice is under-represented in policy. Evidence from 'actually existing' schools (Hattam et al, 2018, p 295), especially those 'at the sharp end' of social and economic inequalities, are dismissed by policy actors or seen as small-scale case studies that cannot be generalised, as the DfE's evidence hierarchy makes explicit. Teachers are positioned as users of research who apply and implement rather than as intellectual workers whose expertise counts in understanding classrooms, and who know how to evaluate research findings and work out their applicability to particular contexts and settings. Thomas (2005), studying the evolution of policy documents in Queensland between 1994 and 2002, suggests that teachers have also been repositioned in policy. While policy documents emphasised (in a positive way) the importance of teachers and teaching, they also increasingly positioned teachers as having low standards and needing improvement and regulation. This positioning limited the extent to which teachers had an 'authoritative voice' in policy, taking them 'out of the equation' in education policy decision making.

The problems that this increasing distance from the substance of educational practice creates for policy making are, we argue, evident throughout this book. Because politicians make big policy choices 'some way away from where the consequences of those choices actually unfold, and indeed without much possibility of understanding what those choices will mean in practice for those they most closely affect' (Moss, 2016, p 939), the unintended or damaging consequences of policies for classroom and school practice are harder to anticipate and more necessary to suppress once they become evident. Because government ministers perceive imperatives for short-term reforms and need personal crash-courses in education before they launch these, they are more likely to draw in an unbalanced way from one particular thinker or 'guru' (as happened in Nick Gibb's case with the work of E.D. Hirsch). Similarly, they are more likely to cherry-pick initiatives from other high-performing countries in response to international rankings, rather than to learn substantive lessons about system design, or to consider how international lessons translate to existing contexts (Lingard et al, 2016). 'Operational disconnect' is a major problem.

Although invisible to most people except those closely connected with policy-making processes, these various shifts and drifts in the way things are done are, we argue, at least as important as the other mistakes discussed in this book. The marginalisation of educational knowledge within education policy has weakened the chances that the right decisions will be made, enabled mistaken policy directions to become entrenched, and weakened the evidence base from which they can be challenged. If policy makers listened more to people who understand how schools and classrooms work, they would understand their evidence base better, and would be wiser in drawing from the experience of other countries, more likely to anticipate the effects of policies on practice and on teachers and learners, and better equipped to avoid unintended policy consequences.

11

Synthetic phonics: a 'perfect storm' of policy mistakes

In Chapters 3, 4 and 5 of this book, we identified three major things that are wrong with our education systems in England and Australia: the dominance of tests; the ways in which the least advantaged children and young people are often least well served by education; and the ways in which the work of teachers and school leaders is changing so that we are making less good use of this valuable resource.

In Chapters 6 to 10, we described five major policy mistakes that have come together to create these problems: a reliance on markets; letting test scores drive policy; over-prescribing teachers' work; misunderstanding educational inequalities; and failing to draw enough on knowledge of education in education policy making. We explained how these big 'wrong turns' have contributed, in combination, to the problems identified earlier.

In this chapter, we sharpen this analysis to show how the mistakes have combined to produce a particular policy, one that currently attracts dispute and controversy in both England and Australia – the practice of synthetic phonics (SP) and the Year 1 phonics check. Unpacking this example in detail helps illuminate what is going wrong and how it might change.

SP and the phonics check

In England and Australia, there have been long-standing concerns that literacy levels are too low, failing to meet the needs of employers. Low literacy achievement is also strongly associated with disadvantage, both in the sense that children from low-income homes are more likely than their more affluent peers to struggle with reading and writing, and in the sense that poor literacy skills hold people back in adult life, perpetuating intergenerational disadvantage. So literacy is often central to ambitions to increase educational equity, social justice and social mobility.

In the past decade in England, and more recently in Australia, a key policy response has been the teaching of reading through SP. Phonics involves the relationship between the sounds in speech and the letter patterns in written words. For example, the sound 'ee' can be represented by the letters 'ea' and also by 'ee', 'ie', 'ei' and 'e'. There are different ways of teaching phonics systematically. SP is a method of teaching in which learners sound out letters and groups of letters and then blend them to make whole words. This is different from another systematic approach, analytic phonics (AP), which introduces whole words first before teaching children to analyse their component parts.

In England, the government has mandated the teaching of reading through SP since 2006, requiring it in teacher training, as part of teacher standards, and through inspection, and making funding available for schools to buy SP programmes and materials. Since 2012, there has been a mandatory phonics check for children in Year 1, in which children have to sound out both real words and pseudo words – strings of letters like 'sut', 'drell' and 'quisk', making it essential that teachers use an SP approach. In Australia, trials of the English Phonics Check were undertaken and evaluated in South Australia (Hordacre et al, 2017) and NSW (Wheldall et al, 2019). In South Australia, the phonics check was mandated in 2018 for children at the end of Year 1. On the question of SP, the current federal Minister for Education has sought 'expert advice on incorporating phonics into the national accreditation standards for initial teacher education' (Tehan, 2019).

Policy effects

According to the government in England, its phonics policy has been a huge success. In 2012, 58 per cent of children passed the Year 1 check. By 2014, this had risen to 74 per cent and by 2016 to 81 per cent, remaining stable since. This rise in 'standards' was the headline message in the education section of the Conservative Party's manifesto for the 2019 general election. Ministers have claimed this means children are reading better, which in turn is developing a love of reading and habit of reading for pleasure (Gibb, 2015b) – claims that have been picked up and reiterated by Australian policy makers (Mitchell, 2020).

However, other evidence suggests we should be cautious. First, reading proficiency levels are not increasing rapidly. The phonics check tests decoding, not reading. For example, it does not test whether children can read common English words (such as 'what' and 'because'), or whether they understand what words mean. Increasing the proportion of young children who can master phonetic decoding does not necessarily mean more will be able to read proficiently. The data bears this out. In England, the cohort of children who took the phonics check in 2014 had a 74 per cent success rate, compared with 58 per cent in 2012. But at the end of Key Stage 1 (KS1) a year later, the proportion assessed as reaching higher levels of reading was only three percentage points higher than for the 2012 cohort at the same point. Four years later, at KS2, there was only one percentage point difference between the cohorts in the proportions achieving expected levels of reading, and two percentage points at high levels. These differences are in line with a continuing upward trend prior to the introduction of the check (DfE 2015, 2019). So, there is a weak relationship between numbers of children passing the phonics check in Year 1 and numbers who acquire reading proficiency when they are a little older. Indeed, this was the conclusion of the government's evaluation of the check, which reported that 'no improvements in attainment or progress that could be clearly attributed to the introduction of the check, nor any identifiable impact on pupil progress in literacy for learners with different levels of prior attainment (Walker et al, 2015, p 67).

Some positive signs are shown in the 2016 Progress in International Reading Literacy Study (PIRLS), the first to test reading comprehension in a cohort of English children who had taken the phonics check. Results revealed a positive correlation between success in the check and achievement in PIRLS (McGrane et al, 2017), but this does not demonstrate that the teaching of SP or the check itself caused later reading success. It could equally well indicate that those children who were deemed good readers at age six went on to develop well, whereas those deemed poor readers on the basis of a decoding test failed to develop their potential as they should have done.

Second, gaps between groups in SP proficiency are not reducing. Since the overall level of success stabilised, there has been a persistent 14 percentage point gap between the success rates of children eligible and not eligible for FSM, and around a 44 percentage point gap between those identified as having a special educational need and not.

Third, research suggests that the check is having the same kinds of effects as the other testing regimes described in Chapters 3 and 7. Time spent preparing for the check is narrowing the curriculum. In England, many children are now introduced to SP as early as two years old, on the basis that getting started early will prepare them better for the check. So formal literacy learning is becoming more dominant in the educational experiences of very young children. The same is beginning to happen in Australia (Campbell et al, 2017). The content of literacy lessons is also becoming more limited as practising for the test (including practising pseudo words) detracts from the development of other reading skills, such as recognising common words and story reading (Clark, 2017). Some popular SP programmes actually discourage the simultaneous use of real books, until letter sounds have been established (Wyse and Styles, 2007). And it appears that the phonics check is also leading to practices of earlier and earlier ability grouping, including in the nursery phase (Bradbury, 2018).

Thus, from the starting point of a widely shared commitment to raising literacy levels and improving equity and social mobility, we seem to have ended up with practices that are narrowing educational experiences and creating earlier within-school segregation, while not improving the relative position of disadvantaged learners and quite possibly not making much difference to reading overall. SP and the phonics check is 'the wrong answer to the right question' (Adoniou, 2017, p 40). So how did we get into this situation?

Evidence-*uninformed* policy making

The story of the adoption of SP and the phonics check is in many ways a classic case of the problems raised in Chapter 10: overemphasis on particular kinds of evidence; the marginalisation of subject specialists and practitioners; and an oppositional rather than a consensual approach.

The turn to SP was made in England in 2006 following the Rose Review commissioned by the New Labour government, which concluded that 'the case for systematic phonic work is overwhelming and much strengthened by a synthetic approach' and that synthetic phonics should be taught 'discretely as the prime approach to establishing word recognition' (Rose, 2006, pp 19, 20). It also concluded that starting SP before age five might be possible and desirable for some children.

As is now well documented, the review gave a good deal of weight to a single study in Clackmannanshire (Johnston and Watson, 2005). This compared SP and AP and reported spectacularly good results for SP, although notably for word recognition, not for reading comprehension. As literacy experts Professors Sue Ellis and Gemma Moss have carefully documented, the study had some methodological limitations, including not taking into account the impact of other school factors (such as teacher effectiveness, access to resources, or other programmes running in the schools), or the ways in which contextual factors (such as parents' reading levels or resources in the home) interacted with the initial intervention. A subsequent analysis of performance in standardised national reading tests does not suggest that reading attainment in the classes exposed to SP was significantly ahead of age-related expectations (Ellis and Moss, 2014). As Gardner (2017) notes, problems with literacy levels in Clackmannanshire were not remedied either in the short term when inspectors noted below average performance compared with similar authorities or in the long term. In 2015, the local authority identified the need to develop 'thinking readers' with higher-order skills.

The point though is not really the limitations of the Clackmannanshire study, but that the evidence it produced was not weighed up with other broader evidence, of which there is an abundance. Major studies from the US (National Institute of Child Health and Human Development, 2000), England (Torgerson et al, 2006), and Australia (DEST, 2005), have looked systematically across the very large body of reading research to synthesise what is known. All of these studies conclude that there *is* evidence in favour of the systematic teaching of phonics, but not in isolation. Phonics should be balanced with other strategies, such as use of rhymes, syllables and whole-word patterns. The latter are particularly useful in the English language, which has many inconsistencies between sounds and letters (Gibson and England, 2016). Goodman and colleagues (2005) also show that meaning can help with decoding, because the context of words sometimes determines how they are pronounced. To identify problem words, children supplement the information from the letters with semantic (meaning) and syntactic (grammar) cues from the surrounding text. In addition, while phonics is important for speedy recognition of many different words, about 100 key words make up about half the words encountered in written English, not all of them phonetically regular or amenable to pictorial representation (such as 'the' or 'said'), so learning these 'sight words' is also important (Clark, 2016).

Teachers know all this. As the Primary English Teachers Association Australia (2015) puts it: 'Expert teachers employ a wide range of teaching strategies based on a deep knowledge of how children learn to read and the needs of learners.' In England, the government evaluation of the phonics check (Walker et al, 2015) found that while 89 per cent of teachers surveyed agreed with the statement 'Phonics should always be taught in the context of meaningful reading', 87 per cent also agreed that 'A variety of different methods should be used to teach children to decode words.' A recent review of meta-analyses on reading instruction (Bowers, 2020) found little or no evidence that systematic phonics was better than the main alternative methods used in schools, including whole language and balanced literacy. Importantly, there is no strong evidence that *synthetic* phonics is any better than any other systematic phonics approach (Wyse and Goswami, 2008).

However, at the time of the Rose Review and subsequently, the government has neither been inclined to take a broad and balanced view of the evidence, nor to seek a consensus between experts from different fields. Indeed, the terms of reference for the Rose Review pointed it to SP, foreshadowing the outcome. Both then and later, evidence supporting the use of *systematic* phonics teaching as part of reading instruction has been used to justify the adoption of the specific approach of SP. The government has also sought to defend this position by creating the impression of a polarised debate between defenders of 'standards', who are backed by scientific evidence, and opponents of phonics, who rely on 'fallacious and unevidenced beliefs about reading instruction' (Gibb, 2017), associated with failed 'progressive' policies of the 1960s and 1970s. Moreover, in tightly enforcing the approach through teachers' standards, initial teacher education and inspection, it firmly locates the problem (low literacy levels) as one of teacher failure to faithfully implement the right approach, thus shifting attention from the design of the policy and from other factors that might be causing the problem (Moss, 2016).

A similar binary has been presented in Australia where the case for the phonics check has been led by the think tank the Centre for Independent Studies (CIS), again with claims to science (Buckingham, 2016, 2017, 2018). Jennifer Buckingham, senior research fellow (CIS) and advocate of the Making Up Lost Time In Literacy (MultiLit) programme, also chaired the expert panel set up in 2017 to provide advice to the education minister regarding the need for a national Year 1 literacy and numeracy check. The six-member panel included the CEO of the Dyslexia SPELD Foundation, head of La Trobe Rural Health, a primary school principal, the director of the Australian Mathematical Sciences Institute and the president of the Australian Association of Mathematics Teachers. The panel concluded that 'there is a role for "light touch" Year 1 screening assessments of literacy and numeracy' and that the 'Year 1 literacy check should focus on phonics' (Buckingham et al, 2017, p 17). It also pointed out that: 'The development and implementation of the checks will be easier in the short-term in relation to literacy, because of the work that has been carried out in England since 2012' (Buckingham et al, 2017, p ii).

Adding to the push for the phonics check from CIS is an evaluation of children's performance on the English phonics check by Wheldall and colleagues (2019). To ensure 'fidelity to the program' (p 140), teachers and school leaders in the three school sites involved received support and training to assist with implementing the check. In addition, the children participating in the test had been instructed in systematic synthetic phonics instruction – MultiLit in this case – in the first two years of school. MultiLit is a research initiative of Macquarie University, has its own research institute and is a private company. The researchers undertaking the evaluation are affiliated with the MultiLit Research Institute. Considering the evaluation in the light of the close relationship between the researchers, MultiLit Pty Ltd and the MultiLit Research Institute, it is perhaps not surprising that it produced positive quantitative data about both SP and the test. But it does more than this. Entwining evidence for the relevance and value of SP (MultiLit) and the test reinforces their enigmatic interdependence, so it is difficult to read this research as an evaluation of the effectiveness of either, nor to draw wider conclusions about the impact on children's reading.

The multiplying effects of policy mistakes

The SP/phonics check policy has arisen from the weaknesses in policy making described in Chapter 10. It is also a product of the failure of policy makers to understand teaching and learning and the causes of educational inequalities (Chapters 8 and 9). In addition, its undesired effects have been magnified because it has been implemented within a marketised system managed by an emphasis on test results (Chapters 6 and 7). As Ball (2017, p 4) says, 'It is the overall effect of multiple changes rather than the specifics of particular changes that is important.'

It may seem odd to say that that phonics policy is not based on an understanding of teaching and learning. Surely that was the whole objective – to replace ineffective teaching with better methods that are tried and tested. Even in those terms, the adoption of SP is flawed. But even if these findings were different, a reliance solely on quantitative studies to test instructional methods is problematic, as discussed in Chapters 8 and 10. This case is a good illustration. In looking solely for 'what works' in teaching reading by testing phonics at age six, the field of vision is restricted to narrow, short-term outcomes and to a small segment of the process of learning to read. The diagnostic and pedagogic skills of teachers are overlooked in favour of fidelity to scripted programmes, and very limited understanding of learning, or of teaching, is applied.

We may know about the science of how children process different kinds of information to make sense of words, but that is not the same as understanding how children learn to read, or how teachers can best teach reading. Reading is not just a skill; it is a social practice. Children read for particular purposes and in particular settings, and their literate practices outside the classroom are important as well as what they do within it. Clearly children need to be taught how to decode printed texts, but decoding in itself is not sufficient to develop competent readers. Freebody and Luke (1990; Luke and Freebody, 1999) provide an expanded definition of reading (and literacy) to include the different resources and strategies readers utilise when they read, respond to, use and analyse texts in sociocultural contexts. And reading is only one interlinked aspect of literacy. Literacy includes writing, speaking and listening, and the use and analysis of text, taking into account its purpose and context (Luke and Freebody, 1999, p 2). Classrooms themselves are social settings in which relationships, values, motivation and engagement are important.

For all these reasons, effective literacy teaching involves understanding and responding to learners' experiences and motivations, as well as understanding and responding to the different ways in which learners use different resources and techniques to make meaning of words. It is not just programme content that matters – the faithful following of a literacy scheme or intervention – but also what teachers do with that content, how they adapt and respond. Louden and colleagues argue that:

> Highly effective literacy teachers do similar activities to their less effective colleagues but achieve greater instructional density; they are more responsive to what children understand, they 'follow-through' teaching points and seize the 'teachable moment'. They are more knowledgeable about their pupils' lives, contextualise their teaching, frame activities to prompt intrinsic purpose and engagement and their teaching has more pace, meta-language and challenge. (Louden et al, 2005, cited in Ellis and Moss, 2014, pp 243–4)

Prescribing only one method of teaching reading ignores all this professional activity. It is, as Ellis and Moss (2014, p 252) put it, 'destructive of forms of professionalism that accept responsibility for reflecting on and adjusting professional practice in the light of research evidence and practitioner experience'. Insisting on programme fidelity and multiple re-sits actually gets in the way of teachers using their professional expertise to address the problems that some children have in learning to read and 'inhibits the search for more productive answers' (Moss, 2016, p 935).

If teachers were able to use the phonics check as it was billed, as a diagnostic tool, their repertoire of teaching practices might not be diminished by the straightjacket of standardisation, and children's early education would not necessarily be dominated by phonics in the way it now seems to be. But the check has become a driver of practice. When the desired outcome is not whether children are reading or making good progress towards reading, but whether they are reaching the expected level on a test of sounding out pseudo words, meaning is distorted. And as Bradbury's study showed, the pressure of the test leads directly to what sociologists Gillborn and Youdell (2000) described as 'educational triage', with school efforts directed intensely towards those children who might pass the test and 'have got to do it or otherwise our score is going to be awful', at the expense of time spent with those who 'aren't going to make it' or 'are going to be fine' (Bradbury, 2018, p 549).

Moreover, markets distort educational practice not just through school-to-school competition but as edu-businesses compete for a share in markets for packaged programmes for teachers to deliver. In the past two decades, private companies and edu-businesses have increasingly stepped into a role that was once the preserve of literacy consultants and curriculum developers in education departments. With government downsizing and outsourcing, publishers such as Pearson and McGraw-Hill now have their own education experts to develop programmes. The explosion of commercial products includes not just teacher instruction manuals, but flash cards, books, videos and DVDs, newsletters, magazines and websites. In the competition for market influence, publishers of educational products are engaged in much more than producing teaching materials and resources. Their reach into what actually transpires in classrooms is increasingly a concern. As Wyse (2003) has demonstrated, in some cases grouping is a direct result of the adoption of particular commercial phonics programmes that require teaching in groups of children at the same phase of phonics development. This is despite the abundant evidence that early ability grouping reduces progress for children who are allocated to lower groups and has 'a profound negative impact on pupils' future social mobility' (Shaw et al, 2016, p 37).

Thus, while politicians frequently argue that efforts to raise levels of early reading are central to closing later gaps in educational attainment and life chances, they miss the fact that the practices they are putting in place to address this might be making inequalities worse. Narrowing teachers' repertoires so that they are focused on decontextualised skill development, labelling and grouping very young children, and putting aside other valued activities to concentrate on early reading are all likely to restrict experiences and marginalise the learners who most need to be included in broad and rich schooling. As Sue Palmer (2016) argues in her book *Upstart*, children who enter nursery settings at two or three years old from the poorest backgrounds may have many disadvantages in terms of physical, cognitive, social and emotional development. But given time and support to explore, play, talk, listen, socialise, feel safe and confident, they still have every chance of educational success. If, on the other hand, their early learning experiences are dominated by formal learning and pressure to achieve age-related norms, they may miss out on these essential foundations of early learning. Palmer notes that among countries that score highly on comparable international tests of literacy are several that do not even start formal schooling until age seven. Instead, literacy skills are learned in a play-based kindergarten stage through activities such as talking and listening, storytelling, songs and rhymes, mark making, painting and drawing, and opportunities to see adults reading and writing for real-life purposes.

So the turn to SP and the phonics check exemplifies in many ways the combinations of misunderstandings and mistakes that produce educational problems and reinforce educational inequalities, in ways exactly opposite to their espoused intentions. It is 'a perfect storm' of policy mistakes. In our final chapter, we turn to what should happen next. How can the perfect storm be avoided in the future?

12

There are alternatives

The end of an era

The educational policies discussed in this book are often described as constituting a distinctive era in which the principles of market liberalism have framed and structured education systems and practices around the world, often in tandem with social and cultural conservatism. A broad political consensus, within and between countries, has supported the development of market-driven systems characterised by standards-based education reforms, test-based accountability, reduced teacher autonomy, and back-to-basics curriculum projects.

This era is coming to a close. In the decade following the 2008 global financial crisis, as the fragility and failure of the neoliberal economic model came into sharp relief, cracks in the educational consensus began to show. Referenced throughout the book, multiple inquiries and reports, including those from parliamentary committees and government-appointed bodies, began to point out that in various ways the twin goals of excellence and equity were not being achieved. England and Australia were not improving in international league tables either of education or economic performance. Places and people were being left behind as governments struggled to manage rapid transitions and shocks fairly, leading to increasing political and social divisions. Social mobility was barely increasing and inequalities in educational experiences and outcomes barely reducing. Social stratification seemed built into systems. Markets and tests were producing more negative than positive effects overall. Schools were becoming less positive and productive places for many young people. Ideas of what might entail a 'fair and equal education' that privileges the interests of all young people in diverse contemporary nations seemed to have been lost (Hattam et al, 2018). In England in 2019, for the first time in decades, the major political parties presented radically different education manifestos, with opposition parties proposing scrapping tests, broadening the curriculum, replacing Ofsted, giving more power to local authorities, preventing the expansion of grammar schools, and taking steps to bring private schools into the state system. In Australia in the same year, at the federal election, Labor tentatively attempted to more firmly distinguish its funding policy from that of the coalition, testing electoral political support for a more needs-based approach to federal funding. It lost too, but the tide was starting to turn in both countries.

Then the global pandemic struck. COVID-19 has triggered new economic conversations, about the valuing of lower paid jobs, the importance of public services, and the extent of regional and ethnic disparities. 'Building back better' and 'levelling up' became the new rhetorics in England, and state interventions to protect jobs and extend eligibility for income support payments were implemented in both England and Australia on a scale not seen since the end of the Second World War. In education, tensions brew between those who advocate the quick resumption of tests and the rapid catch-up of missed learning and those who question whether, if achievements can be assessed by teachers, we need all the apparatus of standardised testing. The social determinants of educational outcomes and the value of schools and teachers have never been more fully recognised. For many parents, the experience of being responsible for maintaining their children's learning at home during periods of lockdown has increased their appreciation of teachers' work. The rapid pivot by teachers to online learning and their role in keeping schools open for the children of essential workers has contributed to a renewed appreciation of the value and importance of the profession to society. Just as the policies of the previous era were a response to the global economic crisis of the 1970s, the current crisis now calls for a new response. If ever there was a time to learn from past mistakes and set a different direction for the future, it is now.

One thing is abundantly clear: if education is really to be better and fairer, policy tweaks will not be enough. We have had policy tweaks. In researching this book, we have come across multiple attempts to mitigate the unwanted consequences of the great mistakes we describe, through changes to funding allocations, regulations, monitoring regimes and incentives. Recent examples in England include reviews of exclusions and the SEN system, working groups on teacher workload, and changes to the Ofsted inspection framework such that it relies less on attainment data. In Australia, changes include recommendations by major reviews, such as a reduced emphasis on end-of-school exams proposed in a review of the NSW curriculum (Masters, 2020), and a move away from a single numeric rank (ATAR) for determining entry levels to university courses, suggested in a national review of secondary pathways (Shergold, 2020). These kinds of changes have the potential to make some difference to some children and young people. There are good policies as well as bad policies. But as long as the system continues to be built on underlying logics that are flawed, these smaller efforts at mitigation and improvement will only go so far.

But is it possible to make more than policy tweaks? Can whole-system reform really be envisaged? International experience suggests that it can. We refer not just to countries such as Finland, Canada and Cuba, which have never gone down the GERM route (Adamson et al, 2016), or to smaller countries that have much more fundamentally repositioned education in relation to wider societal goals, such as Bhutan in its education blueprint for 2014–24 (Ministry of Education, 2014), which reflects the importance of education to the country's goal of improving the 'Gross National Happiness' of its citizens (Thinley, 2016). While we maintain that there is a lot to learn from these systems, many people will find them easy to disregard. The political and social welfare systems of these countries are, after all, very different from those of England and Australia, and the length of time for which they have followed different paths might make them seem just too different to be applicable.

However, there is a bigger movement of change afoot, providing international examples of another kind: countries that did put in place the same kinds of policies as England and Australia but have recently rowed back, or rather started to steer a new course towards better and fairer outcomes. Chile, the pioneer of choice and competition in the early 1980s, recently introduced a Law for School Inclusion, designed to address educational inequalities and school segregation through a suite of reforms including the expansion of state subsidies and the elimination of parental co-payment, for-profit voucher schools and school practices to select students (Valenzuela and Montecinos, 2017). In 2017, New Zealand dropped its National Standards testing system for primary school children, introduced in 2010. Abolishing National Standards, ministers argued that they had become a compliance exercise and a distraction. PISA data also showed that the reading performance of New Zealand's children had fallen since National Standards were introduced (Stuff, 2017; Global Legal Monitor, 2018). Singapore is shifting its focus from exam success to preparing young people with a broader set of skills and knowledge, including human-focused or soft skills like critical thinking, leadership and complex problem solving, and social influence. The changes in Singapore from 2021 come in response to a growing demand for a 'broad-based and well-rounded education' to support students' 'holistic development' (Ministry of Education, 2019). Wales, England's close neighbour, has rejected the English education model, maintaining its comprehensive schools and abolishing league tables. Its education improvement plan puts curriculum development at the centre of its efforts to raise standards, placing demands on teachers to be curriculum actors and to adopt student-centred approaches to learning. It is striking that the rationales for Wales' reforms are not unlike those that underpin English and Australian policies: raising standards, improving literacy and numeracy, breaking the link between disadvantage and educational attainment, and implementing 'what works'. Yet, the approach is starkly different, emphasising learners at the centre, collective responsibility and collaborative relationships between all levels of the schooling system, and the need for teachers to understand and use 'an array of teaching strategies because there is no single, universal approach that suits all situations' (Welsh Government, 2014, p 13).

So things can be different and it is possible to do more than tweak broken systems. In the following section, we offer a basic blueprint for change and some essential preconditions – changes to the way policies are made and evidence used.

Blueprint for change

Regain a wider vision of education. Education is not just about gaining credentials that will produce returns in the labour market. It is not sufficient for education policies to be stated in terms of targets and incentives or punishments and rewards because education is about more than what can be measured. There is a need to recognise that there are broader purposes to schooling than academic attainment and skill acquisition.

Make education for all a fundamental principle for schooling. The practices of schooling must support inclusion not exclusion. Every child has the right to learn and to be supported to reach their potential. Schools should be welcoming and accommodating of all children and families. This means looking hard at practices around admission, behaviour, support and exclusion, and practices such as ability grouping, which should be used in later years, if at all. Most countries with high levels of PISA attainment do not routinely divide children into streams or sets.

Conceptualise inequality in ways that do not blame children and families, since this is not something that they can fix for themselves – it is the fall-out of economic and social inequality and therefore a societal problem not an individual one. **Focus more on equity than attainment gaps.** Think instead in terms of an 'education debt' (Ladson-Billings, 2006) that should be repaid to disadvantaged young people who have been ill served by the system.

Understand education policy more broadly, with reference to areas such as social security, housing and transport, for example (Anyon, 2005). Without this, things that we more typically think of as education policies will struggle to achieve the desired effects. Change the structure of government ministries and cross-departmental working so that ministers have to consider child poverty, health and wellbeing rather than seeing education in isolation. Following Finland's example (Crehan, 2016), equip schools with support teams – dentists, nurses, counsellors and so on – thus investing holistically in preventing problems rather than having to mop them up further down the line. See schools as part of broader integrated service delivery, contributing to community and area regeneration.

Keep levelling the playing field, because the field keeps tilting in ways that mean some children miss out on the benefits of education. This requires an ongoing and systematic redistribution of resources, more than is currently the case in England and much more than in Australia. Additional funding should be allocated not just on a per pupil level with resources targeted at individual children. It should also recognise the organisational demands of very challenging contexts. We need our most experienced teachers working in the most challenging circumstances alongside a range of other professionals who are able to respond to the deep and wide-ranging needs of young people in these contexts. 'Levelling up' requires more than top-ups. It needs substantial and significant ongoing investment.

Build systems for collaboration not competition. This does not necessarily mean abandoning autonomy or choice. Choice per se is not a bad thing among schools that afford different kinds of learning. Providing teachers and communities with the autonomy and resources to develop distinctive approaches to schooling and to supporting diverse learning needs has the potential to allow for a flourishing of innovation and adaptation. But choice should not drive the system so that schools need to compete for students or reputation or results and vastly uneven 'choices' are created between schools of widely different quality and resources. Removing autonomy over admissions and introducing collective local accountability structures would provide the conditions for nearby schools to work together to share expertise and to collaborate in providing linked-up provision to local communities. Restoring greater coordination and public oversight to schools' procurement of goods and services would increase accountability and, in many cases, efficiency.

Reduce the amount of testing and decouple tests from school accountability measures so that 'Systems of assessment … dance to the tune of educational objectives – not to the tune of accountability convenience' (O'Neill, 2013, p 15). This does not mean that standards should be abandoned or that children should not be taught or assessed. Some tests are intended to examine what all students should be able to do and students will attempt them until they achieve mastery. Others are intended to identify differences in what students have learnt and sort them for future study and employment. These are all valid purposes and all of these kinds of tests have widespread support at some level from all kinds of stakeholders in education. **Look at alternative approaches to assessment and accountability that do not distort the activities they are intended to measure,** such as Queensland's approach. Queensland has had a long-established, state-wide, teacher-led system of teacher moderation of student work. Teachers work collaboratively to develop agreements about the kind of performance that counts, across a range of measures. Evaluation has shown that this moderation process is 'viewed positively by both teachers and others within the education community' (Mills and McGregor, 2016b).

Drop the focus on early reading. Not all countries insist on 'early reading'. When formal schooling starts later, children tend to pick up reading quickly, partly because they have better listening skills. A broader conceptualisation of how learning happens suggests that this approach is likely to support 'readers for life' who have a rich enjoyment of texts in different genres. **Abandon the sole emphasis on synthetic phonics for teaching reading, which would remove the need for the phonics check.** This does not mean, however, that children's reading skills would not be checked. Glazzard (2017) proposes that teachers be given professional autonomy to choose from a battery of assessment tools.

Recognise that there is no single proven approach to improving practice. A commitment among educators to working together to modify and contextualise good ideas for local conditions is an excellent place to begin. It is the coming together of these conditions, rather more than the prescription of specific methods and approaches adopted, that is likely to contribute to improvements in the quality of education. There is an important role for governments in supporting, funding and valuing the creation of these conditions in schools.

Be more supportive of teachers and school leaders, since too many are leaving the profession, burnt out and angry with a system that is at odds with their values. We must help teachers reconnect with the reason why most choose to teach – to support the students themselves. Teachers can be a powerful force for change and for good, not just for young people but also for the education systems that many are determined to change. Understanding teachers' work as actively accommodating, subverting and incorporating prescribed pedagogical and assessment practices requires an appreciation of their professionalism, and a rejection of discourses of deficit. Comber (2016) states that we do not usually think of teachers' practices as demonstrating a body of work, perhaps because it is 'sometimes somewhat ephemeral and of the moment' (p 409). Instead, teachers are assumed to translate theory into practice or implement policy. However, Comber's (2016) teacher-researchers demonstrate the nature of a teacher's body of work, or 'oeuvre' (p 409). How might we support teachers to develop their oeuvre? What might the public discourse of schooling look like if it were to be based on a deep respect for teachers, their knowledge and their understanding of the local conditions of teaching and learning?

Preconditions for change

While any of these specific changes is important, the establishment of policy-making processes that are fit for a new era, capable of developing and sustaining a different vision and managing a coherent long-term programme of change is even more so. Putting right mistakes that have developed over 50 years cannot be left to education ministers who are elected for short terms, react in knee-jerk ways to the latest international rankings, need crash courses in educational theory and practice, and are dependent on prominent personally favoured gurus and limited sources of ill-understood evidence. As Moss (2016) puts it, it is time to seek 'common cause' between communities of policy, research and practice: co-determining key questions; inviting critical scrutiny of what works in practice as well as theory; sharing and scrutinising evidence basis from different sources.

There are some clear and practical things on which work could start now. The first is to establish mechanisms for policy makers to draw on a wider range of educational expertise and knowledge. These could include the following measures.

Governments spending their research funds differently. Rather than putting all their eggs in the basket of 'what works' research, they could co-fund broad-based education research institutes, with a mandate and resources to conduct, synthesise and disseminate education research. These could be developed through and with the national professional associations for education researchers (British Educational Research Association and Australian Association for Research in Education) and become seen as the respected go-to place for educational knowledge. Or governments could harness existing expertise in universities, schools and local authorities to existing research organisations, bringing a greater breadth of expertise.

Developing greater learning capacity and depth of knowledge in policy-making processes, through, for example, creating specialist long-term roles within government departments rather than switching civil servants around; establishing secondments and studentships across schools, universities, unions, and governmental organisations; introducing broader processes of consultation and deliberation in policy development. There is also a need to build local and regional collaborations to address educational issues in co-produced ways, sharing data, expertise and practice.

Promoting teacher and expert research further up the evidence hierarchy. Preparing teachers is a process of education, not training. Initial teacher education and professional development could be recast as research-informed processes aimed at developing teachers who have the capacity to conduct research into their own practice, and to utilise educational research to inform their practice. Research production and consumption should be part of the professional work of teachers, with sufficient time allocated to such tasks.

Developing better scrutiny processes to help anticipate and correct the damaging effects of policies. These could include formal governmental processes (as in the case of Wales where all new policy needs to be considered in the light of the well-being of future generations). They could include establishing independent evidence and scrutiny bodies, the educational equivalent of the UK's Office for Budget Responsibility, or enabling practice-based organisations to test decisions against their likely impact in the least advantaged schools or for the least advantaged students. In the absence of government action, universities could self-organise in scrutiny roles, following the example of the National Education Policy Center at the University of Colorado, which convenes a national network of education scholars across the US to comment on educational policy proactively and to write and publish reviews of policy ideas coming from other organisations such as policy think tanks.

Establishing collaborative international mechanisms to learn deeply from other countries. Rather than just responding to PISA results, governments could invest in exchange visits and learning programmes, involving politicians, civil servants, school leaders, teachers, parents and children investigating how things are done differently in other places and the lessons that can be learned. Governmental committees should be properly resourced to learn systematically from policy and practice in other nations.

Yet, these kinds of moves notwithstanding, it is hard to avoid the conclusion that, in formulating their response and recovery to COVID-19 on top of the broad economic and ecological challenges they were already facing, England and Australia both probably need a major once-in-a-generation process of deliberation about the future of their education systems. As we address and emerge from current crises, we need to forge a new consensus on education and a new agenda for educational change.

Doing this will require us to ask different questions about the future than are typically asked in human capital-oriented enquiries, which can become locked into a narrow discussion about the skills needs of the 'fourth industrial revolution', and in future-tech inquiries which challenge us to think about the balance between in-person and online learning and how to ensure equitable access and opportunity in the digital world.

These are important questions that need to be addressed in challenging ways (Adoniou, 2016; Wolfram, 2020).

But the conversation should go well beyond them. It is time again to ask searching questions about what kind of education systems can deliver social justice in the here and now, *and* produce the multiple skills, knowledges and dispositions needed to shape our future societies in more sustainable, resilient, healthy, economically secure and equal ways. And what kind of education systems can help us to accept and respond to the Earth's climate emergency and the 'impending finite-ness of global resources' (Rappleye and Komatsu, 2020, p 190)? Technical questions about system organisation, management and accountability are important, but we need to move beyond them to regain our 'progressive imaginary' (Lingard, 2011, p 355). So we agree with sociologist Professor Ruth Levitas (2013, p xii), who argues for utopia ('the desire for a better way of being or of living') as a method of enquiry, which she calls the imaginary reconstitution of society (IROS). IROS, Levitas argues (2013, p xi), 'facilitates genuinely holistic thinking about possible futures, combined with reflexivity, provisionality and democratic engagement with the principles and practices of those futures'. We think this is what education needs.

To pull it off would require a major effort to change some of the ways we all think, act and react in what have now become bitter and polarised policy conversations. Probably it demands large-scale exercises in rethinking – national commissions or enquiries involving multiple stakeholders and with broad political backing. But it also demands different ways of approaching policy thinking, for all the actors involved. If transformational change is to be achieved, we all need the humility, discipline and imagination to look back as well as forward, dropping the urge to reform and the fear of being seen as 'old fashioned and backward looking' (Lister, 2000, cited in Ball, 2017 p 118). We must be able to acknowledge current policy 'fantasies' (Clarke, 2020), such as that all children can achieve the average or that all parents have equal choices in a system designed to ensure otherwise. At the same time, we should drop critical fantasies:

in which everything would be wonderful if only we could return to some putative golden era of democratic education or if we could just get rid of the elite class of neoliberal policy makers; alas, there was no such golden era while all of us, not just elite policy makers, are complicit in one way or another in the destructive logics of neoliberal education policy. (Clarke, 2020, p 164)

IROS for education would require us to grapple not just with disputed versions of social justice in education (Gewirtz, 1998; Francis and Mills, 2012b) but also some of the real contradictions and dilemmas of making it happen. For example, how can we ensure a strong vocational curriculum offer without sorting people into 'sheep' and 'goats' at an early age on the basis of classed and gendered preconceptions of ability or interest? And how can we enable professional autonomy and curriculum variation while also guaranteeing an entitlement for young people to the same things that their peers enjoy? Tackling these contradictions in an honest way would force us to drop essentialist critiques, such as that everything 'neoliberal' is bad, and that everything is neoliberal, as well as naïve blaming that fails to recognise the fiscal, practical and political constraints of actual policy change. It would make us drop crude binaries, such as assuming that people who are against high-stakes testing are against high standards, and that those who oppose the sole use of synthetic phonics think reading is unimportant. An exercise in IROS would also make us look closely at our assumptions about problems as well as solutions, considering what goes unquestioned when the problem is conceptualised in particular ways and scrutinising why we frame educational problems in the way we do (Bacchi, 2012).

We recognise that the obvious response to such a proposal is that it is impossible. Rarely do national governments work with political opponents and wider constituencies to take stock of whole systems and develop long-term goals and plans. But as Levitas (2013, p xii) writes: 'For those who still think that utopia is about the impossible, what really is impossible is to carry on as we are.' We hope that this book has not only demonstrated very clearly what is wrong, but also that there is solid evidence from multiple and diverse research traditions on which to base a new consensus for change. We are also very aware that consensus is in short supply, while division and conflict are commonplace in a world that is struggling with the immediate threat of a global pandemic and the existential threat to humanity of the climate emergency. There is no greater challenge than shaping the education systems needed for the survival of humanity on our one planet. It will take leadership, the kind of leadership that demonstrates how we might work together for the good of all people. So we have chosen to end this book with a statement by one such leader, New Zealand's Prime Minister Jacinda Ardern, who while delivering an impromptu address to striking teachers in 2018, in which she recognised the value and importance of education systems and teachers in overcoming so many issues and challenges faced by society, acknowledged that when there is a commitment to make things better for children and young people, "there is no you and us, there is only us."

References

Abbott, T. (2013) *The Coalition's Policy for Schools: Students First.* Barton, ACT.

Academies Commission (2013) *Unleashing Greatness: Getting the Best from an Academised System.* London: Pearson and the RSA. Available at: www.educationengland.org.uk/documents/pdfs/2013-academies-commission.pdf [Accessed: 19 February 2019].

ACARA (2019a) *NAPLAN Achievement in Reading, Writing, Language Conventions and Numeracy: National Report for 2019.* Sydney: Australian Curriculum, Assessment and Reporting Authority.

ACARA (2019b) 'What is NAPLAN?', [online]. Available at: www.nap.edu.au/information/faqs/naplan--general [Accessed: 1 February 2019].

Adamson, F., Astrand, B. and Darling-Hammond, L. (eds) (2016) *Global Education Reform: How Privatization and Public Investment Influence Education Outcomes.* New York, NY: Routledge.

Adoniou, M. (2016) 'Literacy standards aren't falling, but they are changing', *The Conversation*, [online] 28 January. Available at: https://theconversation.com/literacy-standards-arent-falling-but-they-are-changing-53626 [Accessed: 24 October 2018].

Adoniou, M. (2017) 'Misplaced faith in synthetic phonics and the Phonics Screening Check', in M. M. Clark (ed.) *Reading the Evidence: Synthetic Phonics and Literacy Learning.* Birmingham: Glendale Education, pp 36–45.

Allen, R. (2007) 'Allocating pupils to their nearest secondary school: the consequences for social and ability stratification', *Urban Studies*, 44(4): 751–70.

Allen, R. (2010) *Does School Autonomy Improve Educational Outcomes? Judging the Performance of Foundation Secondary Schools in England.* DoQSS Working Paper 10-02. London: Department of Quantitative Social Science, Institute of Education.

Allen, R. and Sims, S. (2018) *The Teacher Gap.* Abingdon and New York, NY: Routledge.

Andrews, J. and Perera, N. (2017) *The Impact of Academies on Educational Outcomes.* London: Education Policy Institute. Available at: https://epi.org.uk/publications-and-research/impact-academies-educational-outcomes [Accessed: 12 February 2019].

Andrews, J. and Townley, J. (2017) *The Economic Benefits of Joining a MAT.* London: Education Policy Institute. Available at: https://epi.org.uk/publications-and-research/economic-benefits-joining-establishing-growing-multi-academy-trust [Accessed: 4 May 2020].

Andrews, J., Hutchinson, J. and Johnes, R. (2016) *Grammar Schools and Social Mobility.* London: Education Policy Institute. Available at: https://epi.org.uk/publications-and-research/grammar-schools-social-mobility [Accessed: 29 July 2020].

Andrews, P. and 84 other signatories (2014) 'OECD and Pisa tests are damaging education worldwide – academics', *The Guardian*, [online] 6 May. Available at: www.theguardian.com/education/2014/may/06/oecd-pisa-tests-damaging-education-academics

Anyon, J. (2005) 'What "counts" as educational policy? Notes toward a new paradigm', *Harvard Educational Review*, 75(1): 65–88.

Au, W. (2009) *Unequal by Design: High-Stakes Testing and the Standardization of Inequality.* London: Routledge.

Australian Institute for Teaching and School Leadership (2011) *Australian Professional Standards for Teachers.* Melbourne: AITSL.

Bacchi, C. (2012) 'Why study problematizations? Making politics visible', *Open Journal of Political Science*, 2(1): 1–8.

Bailey, V., Baker, A-M., Cave, L., Fildes, J., Perrens, B., Plummer, J. and Wearring, A. (2016) *Mission Australia Youth Survey Report 2016.* Sydney: Mission Australia.

Baker, J. (2019) 'Seven years after Gonski, why is school funding still inequitable?', *Sydney Morning Herald Digital Edition*, May 17. Available at: https://www.smh.com.au/education/seven-years-after-gonski-why-is-school-funding-still-inequitable-20190516-p51o34.html

Ball, S. J. (1999) 'Labour, learning and the economy: a "policy sociology" perspective', *Cambridge Journal of Education*, 29(2): 195–206.

Ball, S. J. (2003a) *Class Strategies and the Education Market the Middle Classes and Social Advantage*. London: RoutledgeFalmer.

Ball, S. J. (2003b) 'The teacher's soul and the terrors of performativity', *Journal of Education Policy*, 18(2): 215–28.

Ball, S. J. (2017) *The Education Debate*. 3rd edn. Bristol: Policy Press.

Ball, S. J. (2019) 'Australian education policy – a case of global education reform hyperactivity', *Journal of Education Policy*, 34(6): 747.

Ball, S. J. and Junemann, C. (2012) *Networks, New Governance and Education*. Bristol: Policy Press.

Barber, M., Moffitt, A. and Kihn, P. (2010) *Deliverology 101: A Field Guide For Educational Leaders*. Thousand Oaks, CA: Corwin.

Baroutsis, A. and Lingard, B. (2018) 'PISA-shock: how we are sold the idea our PISA rankings are shocking and the damage it is doing to schooling in Australia', *EduResearch Matters*, [blog] 18 February. Available at: www.aare.edu.au/blog/?p=2714 [Accessed: 1 June 2020].

Battellino, R. (2010) 'Twenty years of economic growth', RBA, [online] 20 August. Available at: www.rba.gov.au/speeches/2010/sp-dg-200810.html

Beatty, C. and Fothergill, S. (2018) *The Contemporary Labour Market in Britain's Older Industrial Towns*. Sheffield: Sheffield Hallam University.

Beck, J. (2009) 'Appropriating professionalism: restructuring the official knowledge base of England's "modernised" teaching profession', *British Journal of Sociology of Education*, 30(1): 3–14.

Bennett, T. (2013) *Teacher Proof*. 1st edn. London and New York, NY: Routledge.

Berliner, D. (2011) 'Rational responses to high stakes testing: the case of curriculum narrowing and the harm that follows', *Cambridge Journal of Education*, 41(3): 287–302.

Block, K., Cross, S., Riggs, E. and Gibbs, L. (2014) 'Supporting schools to create an inclusive environment for refugee students', *International Journal of Inclusive Education*, 18(12): 1337-55.

Boaler, J. and Wiliam, D. (2001) 'Setting, streaming and mixed-ability teaching', in J. Dillon and M. Maguire (eds) *Becoming a Teacher*. 2nd edn. Maidenhead: Open University Press, pp 173–81.

Bolton, P. (2010) *National Challenge Schools: Statistics*. Standard Note SN/SG/5062. London: House of Commons Library. Available at: https://dera.ioe.ac.uk/22801/1/SN05062.pdf [Accessed: 1 June 2020].

Bonnor, C. and Shepherd, B. (2017) *Losing the Game: State of our Schools*. Sydney: Centre for Policy Development.

Bowers, J. (2020) 'Reconsidering the evidence that systematic phonics is more effective than alternative methods of reading instruction', *Educational Psychology Review*, 32: 681–705.

Bradbury, A. (2018) 'The impact of the Phonics Screening Check on grouping by ability: a "necessary evil" amid the policy storm', *British Educational Research Journal*, 44(4): 539–56.

Bright, G. (2011) '"Off the model": resistant spaces, school disaffection and "aspiration" in a former coal-mining community', *Children's Geographies*, 9(1): 63–78.

British Humanist Association and Fair Admissions Campaign (2015) *An Unholy Mess: How Virtually all Religiously Selective State Schools in England are Breaking the Law*. London: Fair Admissions Campaign. Available at: https://fairadmissions. org.uk/wp-content/uploads/2015/09/An-Unholy-Mess.pdf [Accessed: 31 May 2020].

Brown, L. (2020) 'Demanding attention, calling for resolution: response to "inequalities in the private funding of public schools: parent financial contributions and socioeconomic status"', *Journal of Educational Administration and History*, 52(1): 60–2.

Buckingham, J. (2016) *Focus on Phonics: Why Australia Should Adopt the Year 1 Phonics Check*. Sydney: Centre for Independent Studies. Available at: www.researchgate.net/publication/311228044_Focus_on_Phonics_Why_Australia_Should_Adopt_the_Year_1_Phonics_Check

Buckingham, J. (2017) 'Why we need the Phonics Check', Centre for Independent Studies, [online] 22 September. Available at: www.cis.org.au/commentary/ideas-the-centre/archive/ideas-80-2017 [Accessed: 23 July 2020].

Buckingham, J. (2018) 'The fight for phonics in early years reading', Centre for Independent Studies, [online] 10 July. Available at: www.cis.org.au/commentary/articles/the-fight-for-phonics-in-early-years-reading [Accessed: 23 July 2020].

Buckingham, J., Nayton, M., Snow, P., Capp, S., Prince, G. and McNamara, A. (2017) *National Year 1 Literacy and Numeracy Check. Expert Advisory Panel: Advice to the Minister*. Canberra: Department of Education and Training.

Burgess, S., Briggs, A., McConnell, B. and Slater, H. (2006) *School Choice in England: Background Facts*. Working Paper 06/159. Bristol: Centre for Market and Public Organisation, University of Bristol.

Burgess, S., Wilson, D. and Worth, J. (2011) *A Natural Experiment in School Accountability: The Impact of School Performance Information on Pupil Progress and Sorting*. Bristol: Centre for Market and Public Organisation, University of Bristol.

Business Council of Australia (2018) *Future-proof Australia's Future Post-Secondary Education and Skills System*. Melbourne: Business Council of Australia. Available at: https://www.bca.com.au/future_proof_australia_s_future_post_secondary_education_and_skills_system

Byrne, B. and Tona, C. D. (2014) 'Multicultural desires? Parental negotiation of multiculture and difference in choosing secondary schools for their children', *The Sociological Review*, 62(3): 475–93.

Caldwell, B. J. (2016) 'Impact of school autonomy on student achievement: cases from Australia', *International Journal of Educational Management*, 30(7): 1171-87.

Caldwell, B. J. and Hayward, D. (1998) *The Future of Schools*. London: Routledge.

Caldwell, B. J. and Spinks, J. (1988) *The Self-Managing School*. London: Routledge.

Campbell, S., Torr, S. and Cologon, K. (2017) 'Ants, apples and the ABCs: the use of commercial phonics programmes in prior-to-school children's services', *Journal of Early Childhood Literacy*, 12(4): 367–88.

Carlisle, E., Fildes, J., Hall, S., Perrens, B., Perdriau, A. and Plummer, J. (2019) *Mission Australia Youth Survey Report 2019*. Sydney: Mission Australia.

Carlson, D. (2005) 'Hope without illusion: telling the story of democratic educational renewal', *International Journal of Qualitative Studies in Education*, 18(1): 21-45.

Centre for Program Evaluation and Shelby Consulting (2013) *Evaluation of the Independent Public Schools Initiative: Final Report*. Perth: Department of Education, Western Australia.

Cheng, S. C. and Gorard, S. (2010) 'Segregation by poverty in secondary schools in England 2006–2009: a research note', *Journal of Education Policy*, 25(3): 415–18.

Children's Commissioner (2019) *Skipping School: Invisible Children. How Children Disappear from England's Schools*. London: Office of the Children's Commissioner. Available at: www.childrenscommissioner.gov.uk/report/skipping-school-invisible-children/ [Accessed: 21 March 2020].

Children's Worlds (2016) *Children's Views on their Lives and Well-Being in 17 Countries: Key Messages From Each Country*. Jacobs Foundation. Available at: http://isciweb.org/_Uploads/dbsAttachedFiles/KeyMessagesfromeachcountry_final.pdf [Accessed: 21 February 2020].

Cirin, R. (2014) *Do Academies Make Use of Their Autonomy?*. London: Department for Education.

Clark, M. M. (2016) *Learning to be Literate: Insights from Research for Policy and Practice*. Abingdon: Routledge.

Clark, M. M. (2017) 'Learning to be literate: what is the evidence?', in M. M. Clark (ed.) *Reading the Evidence: Synthetic Phonics and Literacy Learning*. Birmingham: Glendale Education, pp 1–15.

Clarke, M. (2020) 'Eyes wide shut: the fantasies and disavowals of education policy', *Journal of Education Policy*, 35(2): 151–67.

Clegg, N., Allen, R., Fernandes, S., Freedman, S. and Kinnock, S. (2017) *Commission on Inequality in Education*. London: Social Market Foundation.

COAG (Council of Australian Governments) (2007) 'Council of Australian Governments' meeting 20 December Communique'. Melbourne: Council of Australian Governments.

Comber, B. (2006) 'Pedagogy as work: educating the next generation of literacy teachers', *Pedagogies: An International Journal*, 1(1): 59–67.

Comber, B. (2012) 'Mandated literacy assessment and the reorganisation of teachers' work: federal policy, local effects', *Critical Studies in Education*, 53(2): 119–36.

Comber, B. (2016) 'Poverty, place and pedagogy in education: research stories from front-line workers', *The Australian Educational Researcher*, 43(4): 393-417.

Comber, B. (2017) 'Literacy, geography and pedagogy: imagining translocal research alliances for educational justice', *Literacy Research: Theory, Method, and Practice*, 66(1): 53–72.

Comber, B. and Nixon, H. (2009) 'Teachers' work and pedagogy in an era of accountability', *Discourse: Studies in the Cultural Politics of Education*, 30(3): 333–45.

Comber, B. and Woods, A. (2016) 'Literacy teacher research in high-poverty schools: why it matters', in J. Lampert, and B. Burnett (eds) *Teacher Education for High Poverty Schools*. Cham: Springer International Publishing, pp 193–210.

Connell, R. W. (1992) 'Citizenship, social justice and curriculum', *International Studies in Sociology of Education*, 2(2):133–46.

Connell, R. (2012) 'Just education', *Journal of Education Policy*, 27(5): 681–3.

Connolly, P., Taylor, B., Francis, B., Archer, L., Hogden, J., Mazerod, A. and Tereshchenko, A. (2019) 'The misallocation of students to academic sets in maths: a study of secondary schools in England', *British Educational Research Journal*, 45(4): 873–97.

Considine, G. (2012) *Neo-Liberal Reforms in NSW Public Secondary Education: What has Happened to Teachers' Work?* Sydney: University of Sydney.

Cooper, K. and Stewart, K. (2013) *Does Money Affect Children's Outcomes: A Systematic Review*. York: Joseph Rowntree Foundation.

Cooper, K. and Stewart, K. (2017) *Does Money Affect Children's Outcomes: An Update*. CASEpaper 203. London: Centre for Analysis of Social Exclusion, LSE.

CooperGibson Research (2018) *Factors Affecting Teacher Retention: Qualitative Investigation*. DFE-RR784. London: DfE.

Courtney, S. and Gunter, H. (2015) 'Get off my bus! School leaders, vision work and the elimination of teachers', *International Journal of Leadership in Education*, 18(4): 395–417.

Cranston, N. (2013) 'School leaders leading: professional responsibility not accountability as the key focus', *Educational Management Administration and Leadership*, 41(2): 129–42.

Crehan, L. (2016) *Cleverlands*. London: Unbound.

Crowther, D., Cummings, C., Dyson, A. and Millward, A. (2003) *Schools and Area Regeneration*. Bristol: Policy Press for the Joseph Rowntree Foundation.

Dadds, M. (1997) 'Continuing professional development: nurturing the expert within', *Journal of In-Service Education*, 23(1): 31–8.

Davies, N. (1999) 'Political coup bred educational disaster', *The Guardian*, [online] 16 September. Available at: www.theguardian.com/uk/1999/sep/16/nickdavies [Accessed: 12 August 2018].

Deloitte (2017) *Principal Workload and Time Use Study*. Sydney: NSW Department of Education.

DEST (Department of Education, Science and Training) (2003) *Australia's teachers: Australia's future. Advancing Innovation, Science, Technology and Mathematics* Canberra: Committee for the Review of Teaching and Teacher Education, October. Available at: https://research.acer.edu.au/tll_misc/1/

DEST (2005) *Teaching Reading: National Inquiry into the Teaching of Reading*. Canberra: Australian Government, Commonwealth of Australia. Available at: https://research.acer.edu.au/tll_misc/5

Department of Foreign Affairs and Trade (2020) 'The importance of services trade to Australia', [online]. Available at: www.dfat.gov.au/trade/services-and-digital-trade/Pages/the-importance-of-services-trade-to-australia.

Department of the Prime Minister and Cabinet (2020) *Closing the Gap Report 2020*. Canberra: Australian Government, Commonwealth of Australia. Available at: https://ctgreport.niaa.gov.au/sites/default/files/pdf/closing-the-gap-report-2020.pdf

DfE (Department for Education) (2010) *The Importance of Teaching: The Schools White Paper 2010*. White Paper Cm 2980. London: The Stationery Office. Available at: www.gov.uk/government/publications/the-importance-of-teaching-the-schools-white-paper-2010 [Accessed: 22 February 2019].

DfE (2011) *Teachers' Standards: How Should they be Used?* London: DfE. Available at: https://assets.publishing.service.gov.uk/government/uploads/system/uploads/attachment_data/file/283567/Teachers_standards_how_should_they_be_used.pdf [Accessed: 26 July 2020].

DfE (2015) *Phonics Screening Check and Key Stage 1 Assessments: England 2015*. Available at: www.gov.uk/government/statistics/phonics-screening-check-and-key-stage-1-assessments-england-2015 [Accessed 31 January 2021].

DfE (2016) *Educational Excellence Everywhere*. London: DfE.

DfE (2017) *Strategic School Improvement Fund Classification of Evidence*. Available at: www.gov.uk/government/publications/strategic-school-improvement-fund-classification-of-evidence [Accessed: 13 July 2020].

DfE (2019) *National Curriculum Assessments: Key Stage 2, 2019 (revised)*. Available at: www.gov.uk/government/statistics/national-curriculum-assessments-key-stage-2-2019-revised [Accessed 31 January 2021].

DfEE (Department for Education and Employment) (2001) *Schools: Building on Success: Raising Standards, Promoting Diversity, Achieving Results*. London: DfEE. Available at: www.gov.uk/government/publications/schools-building-on-success-raising-standards-promoting-diversity-achieving-results [Accessed: 19 February 2019].

DfES (Department for Education and Skills) (2003) *Excellence and Enjoyment: A Strategy for Primary Schools*. London, DfES.

DfES (2005) *Higher Standards, Better Schools for All: More Choice for Parents and Pupils*. White Paper Cm 2677. London: The Stationery Office. Available at: www.educationengland.org. uk/documents/pdfs/2005-white-paper-higher-standards.pdf [Accessed: 22 February 2019].

Dorling, D. (2018) *Peak Inequality: Britain's Ticking Time Bomb*. Bristol: Policy Press.

Dracup, T. (2014) 'The politics of setting', *Gifted Phoenix*, [online] 12 November. Available at: https://giftedphoenix. wordpress.com/2014/11/12/the-politics-of-setting [Accessed: 13 May 2020].

Education Council (2014) 'National evidence institute'. Available at: www.educationcouncil.edu.au/National%20 evidence%20institute.aspx

Education Datalab (2016) *Seven Things You Might Not Know About Our Schools*. London: Education Datalab.

Education Endowment Foundation (2015) *Teaching and Learning Toolkit*. London: Education Endowment Foundation. Available at: https://educationendowmentfoundation.org.uk/evidence-summaries/teaching-learning-toolkit [Accessed: 13 May 2020].

Education Policy Institute (2019) *Education in England: Annual Report 2019*. London: Education Policy Institute.

Education Standards Authority (2020) *HSC Course and Performance Band Descriptors*. Sydney: NSW Government. Available at: www.boardofstudies.nsw.edu.au/bos_stats/hsc-pbds.html [Accessed: 20 October 2020].

Edwards, D. and Potts, A. (2008) 'What is literacy? Thirty years of Australian literacy debates (1975–2005)', *Paedagogica Historica*, 44(1–2): 123–35.

Egan, D. (2018) 'Shifting paradigms: Can education compensate for society?', in S. Gannon, R. Hattam and W. Sawyer (eds) *Resisting Educational Inequality: Reframing Policy and Practice in Schools Serving Vulnerable Communities*. Abingdon, Oxon; New York, NY: Routledge, pp 236–244.

Elliott, V., Baird, J-A., Hopfenbeck, T.,Ingram, J., Thompson, I., Usher, N., Zantout, M., Richardson, J. and Coleman, R. (2016) *A Marked Improvement?: A Review of the Evidence on Written Marking*. London: Education Endowment Foundation, p. 35.

Ellis, S. and Moss, G. (2014) 'Ethics, education policy and research: the phonics question reconsidered', *British Educational Research Journal*, 40(2): 241–60.

Ellis, V., Frederick, K., Gibbons, S., Maguire, M., Messer,A., Spendlove, D. and Turvey, K. (2017) *Teacher Development 3.0: How we can transform the professional education of teachers.* London: Teacher Education Exchange. Available at: https://cris.brighton.ac.uk/ws/portalfiles/portal/482814/teacherdevelopmentthreepointzero.pdf [Accessed: 20 May 2020].

ESFA (Education and Skills Funding Agency) (2019) 'ESFA letters to academy trusts about high pay', GOV.UK, [online]. Available at: www.gov.uk/government/publications/esfa-letters-to-academy-trusts-about-high-pay [Accessed: 4 May 2020].

Espeland, W. and Stevens, M. (2008) 'A sociology of quantification', *European Journal of Sociology/Archives Européennes de Sociologie*, 49(3): 401–36.

Ewing, R., Smith, D., Anderson, M. Gibson, R. and Manuel, J. (2004) *Teachers as Learners: Australian Government Quality Teacher Program 'Action Learning for School Teams' Project Evaluation Report.* Sydney: Faculty of Education and Social Work, University of Sydney. Available at: www.researchgate.net/publication/309195456_Teachers_as_learners_Australian_Government_quality_teacher_program_'Action_learning_for_school_teams'_project_evaluation_report/link/58074c0e08aeb85ac86049a6/download

Eyles, A., Hupkau, C. and Machin, S. (2016) 'Academies, charter and free schools: do new school types deliver better outcomes?', *Economic Policy*, 31(87): 453–501.

Firth, B., Melia, V., Bergan, D. and Whitby, L. (2014) '"No ceiling on achievement": breaking the glass ceiling or hitting a steel plate in urban schools?', *The Urban Review Special Issue: Raising Teachers' Voice on Achievement in Urban Schools in England*, 46(5): 877–90.

Fitzgerald, S., Stacey, M., McGrath-Champ, S., Parding, K. and Rainnie, A. (2018) 'Devolution, market dynamics and the Independent Public School initiative in Western Australia: 'winning back' what has been lost?', *Journal of Education Policy*, 33(5): 662–81.

Ford, M. (2013) 'Achievement gaps in Australia: what NAPLAN reveals about education inequality in Australia', *Race Ethnicity and Education*, 16(1): 80–102.

Foster, D. (2019) *Teacher Recruitment and Retention in England*. Briefing Paper 7222. London: House of Commons Library. Available at: https://researchbriefings.parliament.uk/ResearchBriefing/Summary/CBP-7222#fullreport.

Francis, B. and Mills, M. (2012a) 'Schools as damaging organisations: instigating a dialogue concerning alternative models of schooling', *Pedagogy, Culture & Society*, 20(2): 251–71.

Francis, B. and Mills, M. (2012b) 'What would a socially just education system look like?', *Journal of Education Policy*, 27(5): 577–85.

Francis, B., Archer, L., Hogden, J., Pepper, D., Taylor, B. and Travers, M-C. (2017a) 'Exploring the relative lack of impact of research on "ability grouping" in England: a discourse analytic account', *Cambridge Journal of Education*, 47(1): 1–17.

Francis, B., Connolly, P. Hodgen, J., Mazenod, A., Pepper, D., Sloan, S., Taylor, B., Tereshchenko, A. and Travers, M-C. (2017b) 'Attainment grouping as self-fulfilling prophesy? A mixed methods exploration of self confidence and set level among Year 7 students', *International Journal of Educational Research*, 86: 96–108.

Francis, B., Mills, M. and Lupton, R. (2017c) 'Towards social justice in education: contradictions and dilemmas', *Journal of Education Policy*, 32(4): 414–31.

Fraser, N. (1997) *Justice Interruptus: Critical Reflections on the 'Postsocialist' Condition*. London: Routledge.

Freebody, P. and Luke, A. (1990) 'Literacies' programs: debates and demands in cultural context', *Prospect*, 5(3): 85–94.

Gardner, P. (2017) 'The policing and politics of early reading', in M. M. Clark (ed.) *Reading the Evidence: Synthetic Phonics and Literacy Learning*. Birmingham: Glendale Education, pp 26–35.

Garner, J. (2014) 'Schools are becoming "exam factories" which don't equip students for the world of work, claims CBI', *The Independent*, Friday 17 January. Available at: www.independent.co.uk/news/education/education-news/schools-are-becoming-exam-factories-which-don-t-equip-students-world-work-claims-cbi-9067650.html

Gewirtz, S. (1998) 'Conceptualizing social justice in education: mapping the territory', *Journal of Education Policy*, 13(4): 469–84.

Gewirtz, S., Maguire, M., Neumann, E. and Towers, E. (2019) 'What's wrong with "deliverology"? Performance measurement, accountability and quality improvement in English secondary education', *Journal of Education Policy*. DOI: 10.1080/02680939.2019.1706103.

Gibb, N. (2015a) 'How E. D. Hirsch came to shape UK government policy', in J. Simons and N. Porter (eds) *Knowledge and the Curriculum: A Collection of Essays to Accompany E. D. Hirsch's Lecture at Policy Exchange*. London: Policy Exchange.

Gibb, N. (2015b) 'Speech: Nick Gibb: the importance of phonics', GOV.UK, [online] 28 March. Available at: www.gov.uk/government/speeches/nick-gibb-the-importance-of-phonics [Accessed: 8 April 2020].

Gibb, N. (2017) 'Speech: Nick Gibb: the importance of vibrant and open debate in education', GOV.UK, [online] 11 September. Available at: https://dera.ioe.ac.uk/29979/1/Nick%20Gibb_%20The%20importance%20of%20vibrant%20and%20open%20debate%20in%20education%20-%20GOV.UK.pdf [Accessed: 8 April 2020].

Gibbons, S., Machin, S. and Silva, O. (2008) 'Choice, competition, and pupil achievement', *Journal of the European Economic Association*, 6(4): 912-47.

Gibson, H. and England, J. (2016) 'The inclusion of pseudowords within the Year One Phonics "Screening Check" in English primary schools', *Cambridge Journal of Education*, 46(4): 491–507.

Gibson, S., Oliver, L. and Dennison, M. (2015) *Workload Challenge: Analysis of Teacher Consultation Responses*. DFE-RR445. London: DfE.

Gillborn, D. and Youdell, D. (2000) *Rationing Education: Policy, Practice, Reform and Equity*. Buckingham and Philadelphia, PA: Open University Press.

Glazzard, J. (2017) 'What could replace the phonics screening check?', in More than a Score (ed.) *Beyond the Exam Factory: Alternatives to High Stakes Testing*. Northampton: More than a Score, pp 96–101.

Global Legal Monitor (2018) *New Zealand: Education Bill Removes National Standards and Charter School Model from Law*. Available at: www.loc.gov/law/foreign-news/article/new-zealand-education-bill-removes-national-standards-and-charter-school-model-from-law [Accessed: 28 October 2020].

Goldacre, B. (2013) *Building Evidence into Education*. London: DfE.

Goldstein, H. and Noden, P. (2003) 'Modelling social segregation', *Oxford Review of Education*, 29(2): 225–37.

Gonski, D., Arcus, T., Boston, K., Gould, V., Johnson, W., O'Brien, L., Perry, L. A. and Roberts, M. (2018) *Through Growth to Achievement: Report of the Review to Achieve Educational Excellence in Australian Schools*. Canberra: Department of Education and Training. Available at: https://www.dese.gov.au/school-funding/resources/review-funding-schooling-final-report-december-2011

Gonski, D., Boston, K., Greiner, K., Lawrence, C., Scales, B. and Tannock, P. (2011) *Review of Funding for Schooling: Final Report*. Canberra: Department of Education, Employment and Workplace Relations. Available at: file:///Users/dhay2248/Downloads/review-of-funding-for-schooling-final-report-dec-2011.pdf

Goodman, Y. M., Watson, D. J. and Burke, C. L. (2005) *Reading Miscue Inventory: From Evaluation to Instruction*. Katonah, NY: Richard C. Owen.

Gorard, S. (2014) 'The link between academies in England, pupil outcomes and local patterns of socio-economic segregation between schools', *Research Papers in Education*, 29(3): 268–84.

Gorard, S. and Siddiqui, N. (2018) 'Grammar schools in England: a new analysis of social segregation and academic outcomes', *British Journal of Sociology of Education*, 39(7): 909–24.

Gorard, S., Hordosy, R. and See, B. H. (2013) 'Narrowing down the determinants of between-school segregation: an analysis of the intake to all schools in England, 1989–2011', *Journal of School Choice*, 7(2): 182–95.

Gorard, S., Taylor, C. and Fitz, J. (2003) *Schools, Markets and Choice*. London: RoutledgeFalmer.

Gove, M. (2013) 'I refuse to surrender to the Marxist teachers hell-bent on destroying our schools', *Daily Mail*, 23 March. Available at: www.dailymail.co.uk/debate/article-2298146/I-refuse-surrender-Marxist-teachers-hell-bent-destroying-schools-Education-Secretary-berates-new-enemies-promise-opposing-plans.html [Accessed 29 July 2020].

Graham, L. (2018) 'Expanding suspension powers for schools is harmful and ineffective', *The Conversation*, [online] 13 November. Available at: https://theconversation.com/expanding-suspension-powers-for-schools-is-harmful-and-ineffective-106525

Greany, T. and Scott, J. (2014) *Conflicts of Interest in Academy Sponsorship Arrangements: A Report for the Education Select Committee*. London: Institute of Education, University of London. Available at: https://www.academia.edu/30351035/Conflicts_of_interest_in_academy_sponsorship_arrangements_A_report_for_the_Education_Select_Committee [Accessed: 4 May 2020].

Gunter, H., Grimaldi, E., Hall, D. and Serpieri, R. (eds) (2016) *New Public Management and the Reform of Education: European Lessons for Policy and Practice*. London and New York, NY: Routledge. Available at: www.routledge.com/New-Public-Management-and-the-Reform-of-Education-European-lessons-for/Gunter-Grimaldi-Hall-Serpieri/p/book/9781138833814 [Accessed: 27 October 2020].

Gunter, H., Hall, D. and Mills, C. (2015) 'Consultants, consultancy and consultocracy in education policymaking in England', *Journal of Education Policy*, 30(4): 518–39.

Haberman, M. (1991) 'The pedagogy of poverty versus good teaching', *The Phi Delta Kappan*, 73(4): 290–4.

Hallam, S. and Parsons, S. (2003) 'Ability grouping in the primary school: a survey', *Educational Studies*, 29(1): 69–83.

Hallam, S. and Parsons, S. (2013) 'Prevalence of streaming in UK primary schools: evidence from the Millennium Cohort Study', *British Educational Research Journal*, 39(3): 514–44.

Halsey, J. (2018) *Independent Review into Regional, Rural and Remote Education: Final Report*. Canberra: Department of Education and Training. Available at: www.education.gov.au/independent-review-regional-rural-and-remote-education

Hardy, I. (2015) 'A logic of enumeration: the nature and effects of national literacy and numeracy testing in Australia', *Journal of Education Policy*, 30(3): 335–62.

Harris, P., Turbill, J., Kervin, L. and Harden-Thew, K. (2010) 'Mapping the archive: an examination of research reports in AJLL 2000-2005', *Australian Journal of Language and Literacy*, 33(3): 173–96.

Hattam, R. and Every, D. (2010) 'Teaching in fractured classrooms : refugee education, public culture, community and ethics', *Race, Ethnicity and Education*, 13(4): 409-424.

Hattam, R., Sawyer, W. and Gannon, S. (2018) 'Reclaiming educational equality: towards a manifesto', in S. Gannon, R. Hattam and W. Sawyer (eds) *Resisting Educational Inequality: Reframing Policy and Practice in Schools Serving Vulnerable Communities*. Abingdon and New York, NY: Routledge, pp 294–9.

Hattie, J. (2009) *Visible Learning: A Synthesis of Over 800 Meta-Analyses Relating to Achievement*. Abingdon: Routledge.

Hayes, D., Mills, M., Christie, P. and Lingard, B. (2005) *Teachers and Schooling Making a Difference: Productive Pedagogies, Assessment and Performance*. Sydney: Allen and Unwin.

Hayes, D., Hattam, R., Comber, B., Kerkham, L., Lupton, R. and Thomson, P. (2017) *Literacy, Leading and Learning: Beyond Pedagogies of Poverty*. Abingdon and New York, NY: Routledge.

Hempel-Jorgensen, A. (2009) 'The construction of the "ideal pupil" and pupils' perceptions of "misbehaviour" and discipline: contrasting experiences from a low-socio-economic and a high-socio-economic primary school', *British Journal of Sociology of Education*, 30(4): 435–48.

Hempel-Jorgensen, A., Cremin, T., Harris, D. and Chamberlain, L. (2018) 'Pedagogy for reading for pleasure in low socio-economic primary schools: beyond "pedagogy of poverty"?', *Literacy*, 52(2): 86–94.

Hofkins, D. and Northen, S. (eds) (2009) *Introducing the Cambridge Primary Review*. Cambridge: Faculty of Education, University of Cambridge.

Holloway, J. and Keddie, A. (2020) 'Competing locals in an autonomous schooling system: the fracturing of the "social" in social justice', *Educational Management Administration & Leadership*, 48(5): 786–801.

Hordacre, A.-L., Moretti, C. M. and Spoehr, J. (2017) *Evaluation of the Trial of the UK Phonics Screening Check in South Australian Schools*. Clovelly Park: Australian Industrial Transformation Institute, Flinders University.

Horgan, G. (2007) *The Impact of Poverty on Young Children's Experience of School*. York: Joseph Rowntree Foundation.

House of Commons Children, Schools and Families Committee (2008) *Testing and Assessment: Third Report of Session 2007–08*. HC 269-I. London: The Stationery Office. Available at: https://publications.parliament.uk/pa/cm200708/cmselect/cmchilsch/169/169.pdf [Accessed: 18 January 2020].

House of Commons Education Committee (2018) *Forgotten Children: Alternative Provision and the Scandal of Ever Increasing Exclusions: Fifth Report of Session 2017–19*. HC 342. London: House of Commons.

House of Lords Select Committee on Regenerating Seaside Towns and Communities (2019) *The Future of Seaside Towns*. London: House of Lords.

Howell, A. (2015) 'Exploring children's experiences of NAPLAN: beyond the cacophony of adult debate', Unpublished doctoral thesis, University of Queensland.

Howell, A. (2016) 'Exploring children's lived experiences of NAPLAN', in B. Lingard, G. Thomson and S. Sellar (eds) *National Testing in Schools: An Australian Assessment*. London and New York, NY: Routledge, pp 164–80.

Hutchings, M. (2015) *Exam Factories: The Impact of Accountability Measures on Children and Young People*. London: National Union of Teachers.

Hutchings, M., Francis, B. and Kirby, P. (2015) *Chain Effects 2015: The Effect of Academy Chains on Low-Income Students.* London: The Sutton Trust. Available at: www.suttontrust. com/wp-content/uploads/2015/07/Chain-Effects-2015.pdf [Accessed: 12 February 2019].

Inchley, J., Currie, D., Young, T., Samdal, O., Torsheim, T., Augustson,L., Mathison, F., Aleman-Diaz, A., Molcho, M., Weber, M. and Barnekow, V. (eds) (2016) *Growing up Unequal: Gender and Socioeconomic Differences in Young People's Health and Well-Being. Health Behaviour in School-Aged Children (HBSC) Study: International Report from the 2013/2014 Survey.* Copenhagen: World Health Organization Regional Office for Europe.

Independent Teacher Workload Review Group (2016a) *Eliminating Unnecessary Workload Around Marking: Report of the Independent Teacher Workload Review Group.* London: DfE. Available at: www.gov.uk/government/publications/reducing-teacher-workload-marking-policy-review-group-report [Accessed: 3 January 2019].

Independent Teacher Workload Review Group (2016b) *Eliminating Unnecessary Workload Around Planning and Teaching Resources: Report of the Independent Teacher Workload Review Group.* London: DfE. Available at: www.gov.uk/government/publications/reducing-teacher-workload-planning-and-resources-group-report [Accessed: 3 January 2019].

Ingvarson, L. (2010) 'Recognising accomplished teachers in Australia : where have we been? Where are we heading?', *Australian Journal of Education*, 54(1): 46–71.

Jackson, J. and Lamb, S. (2016) *Creating Winners and Battlers: Examining Inequality Between Melbourne Schools.* Melbourne: Centre for International Research on Education Systems, Victoria University.

Jerrim, J. and Sims, S. (2019) *The Teaching and Learning International Survey (TALIS) 2018.* London: DfE.

Johnson, B., Sullivan, A. and Simons, M. (2019) 'How school leaders attract, recruit, develop and retain the early career teachers they want', in A. Sullivan, B. Johnson and M. Simons (eds) *Attracting and Keeping the Best Teachers: Issues and Opportunities.* Singapore: Springer Singapore, pp 101–22.

Johnston, K. and Hayes, D. (2008) '"This is as good as it gets": classroom lessons and learning in challenging circumstances', *Australian Journal of Language and Literacy*, 31(2): 109–27.

Johnston, R. and Watson, J. (2005) *The Effects of Synthetic Phonics Teaching on Reading and Spelling Attainment*. Edinburgh: Scottish Executive. Available at: www.gov.scot/Resource/Doc/36496/0023582.pdf.

Jones, H. (2010) 'National Curriculum tests and the teaching of thinking skills at primary schools – parallel or paradox?', *Education 3-13*, 38(1): 69–86.

Jones, L. and Ploner, J. (2019) 'The restrictive role of the national curriculum and high-stakes testing in the UK City of Culture', Paper presented at British Educational Research Association Conference, University of Manchester, 10–12 September.

Karmel, P. (1985) *Quality of Education in Australia: Report of the Review Committee*. Canberra: Australian Government Publishing Service.

Keating, P. (1994) *Working Nation: Policies and Programs*. Canberra: Australian Government Publishing Service.

Keddie, A. (2016) 'School autonomy as 'the way of the future': issues of equity, public purpose and moral leadership', *Educational Management Administration and Leadership*, 44(5): 713–27.

Kenway, J. (2013) 'Challenging inequality in Australian schools: Gonski and beyond', *Discourse: Studies in the Cultural Politics of Education*, 34(2): 286–308.

Kerr, K. and West, M. (eds) (2010) *Social Inequality: Can Schools Narrow the Gap?*. Macclesfield: British Educational Research Association.

Kim, K. H. (2011) 'The creativity crisis: the decrease in creative thinking scores on the Torrance Tests of Creative Thinking', *Creativity Research Journal*, 23(4): 285–95.

King, A. and Crewe, I. (2014) *The Blunders of our Governments*. London: Oneworld Publications.

Klenowski, V. and Wyatt-Smith, C. (2012) 'The impact of high stakes testing: the Australian story', *Assessment in Education: Principles, Policy & Practice*, 19(1): 65–79.

Kulz, C. (2017) *Factories for Learning: Making Race, Class and Inequality in the Neoliberal Academy*. Manchester: Manchester University Press.

Ladson-Billings, G. (2006) 'From the achievement gap to the education debt: understanding achievement in US schools', *Educational Researcher*, 35(7): 3–12.

Lamb, S. (2007) 'School reform and inequality in urban Australia: a case of residualising the poor', in R. Teese, S. Lamb, M. Duru-Bellat and S. Helme (eds) *International Studies in Educational Inequality, Theory and Policy*. Dordrecht: Springer Netherlands, pp 672–709.

Lamb, S., Jackson, J., Walstab, A. and Huo, S. (2015) *Educational Opportunity in Australia 2015: Who Succeeds and Who Misses Out*. Melbourne: Centre for International Research on Education Systems, Victoria University for the Mitchell Institute.

Lareau, A. (2011) *Unequal Childhoods*. 2nd edn. Oakland, CA: University of California Press.

Lawn, M. (2013a) 'A systemless system: designing the disarticulation of English state education', *European Educational Research Journal*, 12(2): 231–41.

Lawn, M. (2013b) 'Introduction: the rise of data in education', in M. Lawn (ed.) *The Rise of Data in Education Systems: Collections, Visualisation and Use*. Oxford: Symposium Books, pp 7–10.

Leckie, G. and Goldstein, H. (2017) 'The evolution of school league tables in England 1992–2016: "contextual value-added", "expected progress" and "Progress 8"', *British Educational Research Journal*, 43(2): 193–212.

Leigh, A. (2009) 'What evidence should social policy makers use?', *Australian Treasury Economic Roundup*, 1: 27–43.

Levitas, R. (2005) *The Inclusive Society?: Social Exclusion and New Labour*. 2nd edn. Basingstoke: Palgrave Macmillan.

Levitas, R. (2013) *Utopia as Method: The Imaginary Reconstitution of Society*. Basingstoke: Palgrave Macmillan.

Lingard, B. (2011) 'Policy as numbers: ac/counting for educational research', *The Australian Educational Researcher*, 38(4): 355–82.

Lingard, B., Martino, W. Rezai-Rashti, G. and Sellar, S. (2016) *Globalizing Educational Accountabilities*. Abingdon and New York, NY: Routledge.

Lingard, B., Sellar, S., Hogan, A. and Thompson, G. (2017) *Commercialisation in Public Schooling (CIPS): Final Report*. Sydney: New South Wales Teachers Federation.

Linn, R. L. (2001) *The Design and Evaluation of Educational Assessment and Accountability Systems*. Center for the Study of Evaluation Technical Report 539. Los Angeles, CA: University of California. Available at: https://cresst.org/wp-content/uploads/TR539.pdf

Lipman, P. (2004) *High Stakes Education : Inequality, Globalization, and Urban School Reform*. London and New York, NY: RoutledgeFalmer.

Literacy Task Force (1997) *The Implementation of the National Literacy Strategy*, London: Department for Education and Employment.

Liu, Y., Bessudnov, A., Black, A. and Norwich, B. (2020) 'School autonomy and educational inclusion of children with special needs: evidence from England', *British Educational Research Journal*, 46(3): 532–52.

Loughland, T. and Thompson, G. (2016) 'The problem of simplification: think-tanks, recipes, equity and "turning around low-performing schools"', *The Australian Educational Researcher*, 43: 111–29.

Luke, A. and Freebody, P. (1999) 'Further notes on the four resources model', *Reading Online*, pp 1–4.

Lupton, R. (2011) '"No change there then!" (?): the onward march of school markets and competition', *Journal of Educational Administration and History*, 43(4): 309–23.

Lupton, R. and Hayes, D. (2018) 'Think tanks and the pedagogical dispositions and strategies of socially critical researchers: a case study of inequalities in schooling', *Policy Futures in Education*, 16(2): 202–16.

Lupton, R. and Obolenskaya, P. (2013) *Labour's Record on Education: Policy, Spending and Outcomes 1997–2010*. Social Policy in a Cold Climate Working Paper 3. London: Centre for Analysis of Social Exclusion, LSE.

Lupton, R. and Obolenskaya, P. (2020) *The Conservatives' Record on Compulsory Education: Spending, Policies and Outcomes in England, May 2015 to pre-COVID 2020*. SPDO Research Paper 6. London: Centre for Analysis of Social Exclusion, LSE.

Lupton, R. and Thomson, S. (2015) *The Coalition's Record on Schools: Policy, Spending and Outcomes 2010-2015*. Social Policy in a Cold Climate Working Paper 13. London: Centre for Analysis of Social Exclusion, LSE.

Lyons-Lee, B. (2019) 'Why I stopped teaching and why I'm going back', 14 December, *Sydney Morning Herald*, [online] 14 December. Available at: https://www.smh.com.au/lifestyle/life-and-relationships/why-i-stopped-teaching-and-why-i-m-going-back-20191206-p53hhy.html

Machin, S. and Silva, O. (2013) 'School structure, school autonomy and the tail', in P. Marshall (ed.) *The Tail: How England's Schools Fail One Child in Five – And What Can be Done*. London: Profile Books, pp 87–110.

Macqueen, S. E. (2013) 'Grouping for inequity', *International Journal of Inclusive Education*, 17(3): 295–309.

Mason, S. and Matas, C. P. (2015) 'Teacher attrition and retention research in Australia: towards a new theoretical framework', *Australian Journal of Teacher Education*, 40(11): 45–66.

Masters, G. (2020) *Nurturing Wonder and Igniting Passion – Designs for a New School Curriculum: NSW Curriculum Review*. Sydney: NSW Education Standards Authority.

Masters, G. and Forster, M. (1997) *Mapping Literacy Achievement: Results of the 1996 National School English Literacy Survey*. Melbourne: Australian Council for Educational Research.

McCulloch, G. (1993) 'Judgement of the teacher: the Norwood Report and internal examinations', *International Studies in Sociology of Education*, 3(1): 129–43.

McDowell, L. and Bonner-Thompson, C. (2020) 'The other side of coastal towns: young men's precarious lives on the margins of England', *Environment and Planning A: Economy and Space*, 52(5): 916–32.

McGaw, B., Louden, W. and Wyatt-Smith, C. (2020) *NAPLAN Review: Final Report*. State of New South Wales (Department of Education), State of Queensland (Department of Education), State of Victoria (Department of Education and Training), and Australian Capital Territory. Available at: https://naplanreview.com.au/__data/assets/pdf_file/0004/1222159/2020_NAPLAN_review_final_report.pdf

McGrane, J., Stiff, J., Baird, J-A., Lenkeit, J. and Hopfenbeck, T. (2017) *Progress in International Reading Literacy Study (PIRLS): National Report for England*. London: DfE. Available at: https://assets.publishing.service.gov.uk/government/uploads/system/uploads/attachment_data/file/664562/PIRLS_2016_National_Report_for_England-_BRANDED.pdf [Accessed: 15 April 2020].

McGrath-Champ, S., Wilson, R., Stacey, M. and Fitzgerald, S. (2018) *Understanding Work in Schools: The Foundation for Teaching and Learning*. Sydney: New South Wales Teachers Federation.

McGrath-Champ, S., Stacey, M., Wilson, R., Fitzgerald, S., Rainnie, A. and Parding, L. (2019) 'Principals' support for teachers' working conditions in devolved school settings: insights from two Australian states', *Educational Management Administration and Leadership*, 47(4): 590–605.

McGregor, G., Mills, M., te Riele, K., Baroutsis, A. and Hayes, D. (2017) *Re-Imagining Schooling for Education: Socially Just Alternatives*. London: Palgrave Macmillan.

McInerney, P. and Smyth, J. (2014) '"I want to get a piece of paper that says I can do stuff": youth narratives of educational opportunities and constraints in low socio-economic neighbourhoods', *Ethnography and Education*, 9(3): 239–52.

McKenzie, P., Weldon, P., Rowley, G., Murphy, M. and McMillan, J. (2014) *Staff in Australia's Schools 2013: Main Report on the Survey*. Canberra: Department of Education, Australian Government.

McNally, S. (2015) 'Schools: organisation, resources, and effectiveness', in R. Cassen, S. McNally and A. Vignoles (eds) *Making a Difference in Education: What the Evidence Says*. Abingdon and New York, NY: Routledge, pp 57–74.

Millar, F. (2016) 'Forty years after the Ruskin speech, education needs another moment', *The Guardian*, [online] 13 December. Available at: www.theguardian.com/education/2016/dec/13/ruskin-speech-education-jim-callaghan-reforms [Accessed: 24 March 2020].

Mills, M. and McGregor, G. (2016a) *Engaging Students in Engaging Schools: Lessons from Queensland's Alternative Education Sector*. Brisbane: Youth Affairs Network Queensland.

Mills, M. and McGregor, G. (2016b) 'Learning not borrowing from the Queensland education system: lessons on curricular, pedagogical and assessment reform', *The Curriculum Journal*, 27(1): 113–33.

Ministry of Education (2014) *Bhutan Education Blueprint 2014–2024. Rethinking Education.* Thimphu, Bhutan: Ministry of Education, Royal Government of Bhutan. Available at: http://www.education.gov.bt/wp-content/downloads/publications/publication/Bhutan-Education-Blueprint-2014-2024.pdf

Ministry of Education (2019) 'Our students'. Available at: https://beta.moe.gov.sg/education-in-SG/our-students/

Mission Australia (2010) *National Survey of Young Australians 2010: Key and Emerging Issues.* Sydney: Mission Australia.

Mitchell, S. (2020) 'The reading wars are over – and phonics has won', *The Sydney Morning Herald Digital Edition*, November 20. Available at https://www.smh.com.au/national/nsw/the-reading-wars-are-over-and-phonics-has-won-20201127-p56ioj.html

Mockler, N. (2014) 'Simple solutions to complex problems: moral panic and the fluid shift from "equity" to "quality" in education', *Review of Education*, 2(2): 115–43.

Moodie, N., Maxwell, J. and Rudolph, S. (2019) 'The impact of racism on the schooling experiences of Aboriginal and Torres Strait Islander students: a systematic review', *The Australian Educational Researcher*, 46(2): 273–95.

Morris, S., Patel, O., Stainthorp, C. and Stevenson, O. (2019) *Structurally Unsound: Exploring Inequalities – Igniting Research to Better Inform UK Policy.* London: UCL and the Resolution Foundation.

Mortimore, P. (2013) *Education Under Siege: Why There is a Better Alternative.* Bristol: Policy Press.

Moss, G. (2016) 'Knowledge, education and research: making common cause across communities of practice', *British Educational Research Journal*, 42(6): 927–44.

Muijs, D. and Dunne, M. (2010) 'Setting by ability – or is it? A quantitative study of determinants of set placement in English secondary schools', *Educational Research*, 52(4): 391–407.

NASUWT (National Association of Schoolmasters Union of Women Teachers) (2019) *The Big Question 2019: An Opinion Survey of Teachers and Headteachers*. London: NASUWT. Available at: www.nasuwt.org.uk/uploads/assets/uploaded/981c20ce-145e-400a-805969e777762b13.pdf [Accessed: 3 March 2020].

National Institute of Child Health and Human Development (2000) *Teaching Children to Read: An Evidence-Based Assessment of the Scientific Research Literature on Reading and its Implications for Reading Instruction: Reports of the Sub Groups*. Report of the National Reading Panel NIH 00-4754. Washington, DC: US Government Printing Office.

Neighbourhood Renewal Unit (2008) 'Neighbourhood Renewal Unit – departmental floor targets'. Available at: https://webarchive.nationalarchives.gov.uk/20080102110515/http://www.neighbourhood.gov.uk/page.asp?id=585 [Accessed: 1 June 2020].

Neumann, E., Gewirtz, S. Maguire, M. and Towers, E. (2020) 'Neoconservative education policy and the case of the English Baccalaureate', *Journal of Curriculum Studies*, 52(5): 702–19.

Nichols, S., Glass, G. and Berliner, D. (2006) 'High-stakes testing and student achievement: does accountability pressure increase student learning?', *Education Policy Analysis Archives*, 14(1): 1–180.

NSW Ombudsman (2017) *NSW Ombudsman Inquiry into behaviour management in schools: A Special Report to Parliament under s 31 of the Ombudsman Act 1974*. Sydney: NSW Ombudsman.

Nye, P. (2017) 'Who's left: the main findings', *FFT Education Datalab*, 31 January. Available at: https://ffteducationdatalab.org.uk/2017/01/whos-left-the-main-findings [Accessed: 13 November 2018].

Obolenskaya, P. and Hills, J. (2019) 'Flat-lining or seething beneath the surface? Two decades of changing economic inequality in the UK', *Oxford Review of Economic Policy*, 35(3): 467–89.

Obolenskaya, P., Lupton, R. and Provan, B. (2016) *Pulling in the Same Direction? Economic and Social Outcomes in London and the North of England Since the Recession.* Social Policy in a Cold Climate Working Paper 23. London: Centre for Analysis of Social Exclusion, LSE. Available at: http://sticerd.lse.ac.uk/dps/case/spcc/wp23.pdf

OECD (Organisation for Economic Co-operation and Development) (2004) *Learning for Tomorrow's World – First Results from PISA 2003.* Paris: OECD Publishing.

OECD (2017) *PISA 2015 Results (Volume III): Students' Well-Being.* Paris: OECD Publishing. Available at: https://doi.org/10.1787/9789264273856-en

OECD (2018) *Job Creation and Local Economic Development 2018: Preparing for the Future of Work.* Paris: OECD Publishing. Available at: https://doi.org/10.1787/9789264305342-en

OECD (2019) *TALIS 2018 Results: Teachers and School Leaders as Lifelong Learners (Volume I).* Paris: OECD Publishing. Available at: https://read.oecd-ilibrary.org/education/talis-2018-results-volume-i_1d0bc92a-en [Accessed: 3 March 2020].

OECD (2020a) 'Students' self-efficacy and fear of failure', in OECD, *PISA 2018 Results (Volume III): What School Life Means for Students' Lives.* Paris: OECD Publishing, pp 187–198. doi: 10.1787/2f9d3124-en.

OECD (2020b) *Country Note: Programme for International Student Assessment (PISA): Results from PISA 2018. United Kingdom.* Paris: OECD Publishing. Available at: www.oecd.org/pisa/publications/PISA2018_CN_GBR.pdf [Accessed: 18 January 2020].

Ofsted (Office for Standards in Education, Children's Services and Schools) (2013) *The Pupil Premium: How Schools are Spending the Funding Successfully to Maximise Achievement.* London: Ofsted.

Ofsted (2014) *The Pupil Premium: An Update.* London: Ofsted.

Ofsted (2015) *Education and Skills: The Annual Report of Her Majesty's Chief Inspector of Education, Children's Services and Skills 2014/15.* London: Ofsted. Available at: https://assets.publishing.service.gov.uk/government/uploads/system/uploads/attachment_data/file/483347/Ofsted_annual_report_education_and_skills.pdf.

Ofsted (2019a) 'Off-rolling: an update on recent analysis', Ofsted, [blog] 6 September. Available at: https://educationinspection.blog.gov.uk/2019/09/06/off-rolling-an-update-on-recent-analysis [Accessed: 3 March 2020].

Ofsted (2019b) 'Data view', Tableau Public, [online]. Available at: https://public.tableau.com/profile/ofsted#!/vizhome/Dataview/Viewregionalperformanceovertime [Accessed: 13 May 2020].

O'Neill, O. (2013) 'Intelligent accountability in education', *Oxford Review of Education*, 39(1): 4–16.

Ovenden-Hope, T. and Passy, R. (2015) *Coastal Academies: Changing School Cultures in Disadvantaged Coastal Regions in England*. Plymouth: University of Plymouth.

Ovenden-Hope, T. and Passy, R. (2019) *Educational Isolation: A Challenge for Schools in England*. Plymouth: Plymouth Marjon University and University of Plymouth.

Ozga, J. (2009) 'Governing education through data in England: from regulation to self-evaluation', *Journal of Education Policy*, 24(2): 149–62.

Palmer, S. (2016) *Upstart: The Case for Raising the School Starting Age and Providing What the Under-Sevens Really Need*. Edinburgh: Floris Books.

Pampaka, M. and Williams, J. (2016) 'Mathematics teachers' and students' perceptions of transmissionist teaching and its association with students' dispositions', *Teaching Mathematics and its Applications: An International Journal of the IMA*, 35(3): 118–30.

Passy, R. and Ovenden-Hope, T. (2017) 'Class of 2010: a qualitative longitudinal study of an English secondary school that became an academy', SAGE Research Methods Cases Part 2, [online]. Available at: http://methods.sagepub.com/case/qualitative-longitudinal-english-secondary-school-became-academy

Passy, R. and Ovenden-Hope, T. (2020) 'Exploring school leadership in coastal schools: "getting a fair deal" for students in disadvantaged communities', *Journal of Education Policy*, 35(2): 222–36.

Piketty, T. (2014) *Capital in the Twenty-First Century*. Cambridge, MA: Harvard University Press.

Plows, V., Bottrell, D. and Te Riele, K. (2016) 'Valued outcomes in the counter-spaces of alternative education programs: success but on whose scale?', *Geographical Research*, 55(1): 29–37.

Polesel, J. (2008) 'Democratising the curriculum or training the children of the poor: schoolbased vocational training in Australia', *Journal of Education Policy*, 23(6): 615–32.

Polesel, J., Rice, S. and Dulfer, N. (2014) 'The impact of high-stakes testing on curriculum and pedagogy: a teacher perspective from Australia', *Journal of Education Policy*, 29(5): 640–57.

Primary English Teachers Association Australia (2015) 'Approaches to early reading instruction', [online]. Available at: www.petaa.edu.au/w/About/PETAA_position_papers.aspx/#earlyreading [Accessed: 31 August 2018].

Proctor, H. (2011) 'School choice is not the answer to everything', *The Conversation*, [online] 12 July. Available at: https://theconversation.com/school-choice-is-not-the-answer-to-everything-1966

Raffo, C. (2014) *Improving Educational Equity in Urban Contexts*. Abingdon and New York, NY: Routledge.

Ralls, D. (2019) '"Becoming co-operative" – challenges and insights: repositioning school engagement as a collective endeavour', *International Journal of Inclusive Education*, 23(11): 1134–48.

Ramsey, G. (2000) *Quality Matters. Revitalising Teaching: Critical times, Critical Choices. Report of the Review of Teacher Education*. Sydney: New South Wales Department of Education. Available at https://www.det.nsw.edu.au/teachrev/reports/reports.pdf

Rappleye, J. and Komatsu, H. (2020) 'Towards (comparative) educational research for a finite future', *Comparative Education*, 56(2): 190–217.

Ravitch, D. (2011) *The Death and Life of the Great American School System*. New York, NY: Basic Books.

Rayner, S. M. (2017) 'Admissions policies and risks to equity and educational inclusion in the context of school reform in England', *Management in Education*, 31(1): 27–32.

Reay, D. (2017) *Miseducation: Inequality, Education and the Working Classes*. Bristol: Policy Press.

Reid, H. and Westergaard, J. (2017) '"Oh I do like to be beside the seaside": opportunity structures for four un/underemployed young people living in English coastal towns', *British Journal of Guidance & Counselling*, 45(3): 341–55.

Research Schools Network (2020) 'Our aims', [online]. Available at: https://researchschool.org.uk/about/our-aims [Accessed: 15 July 2020].

Rizvi, F. (2013) 'Equity and marketisation: a brief commentary', *Discourse: Studies in the Cultural Politics of Education*, 34(2): 274–78.

Rose, J. (2006) *Independent Review of the Teaching of Early Reading: Final Report.* Nottingham: DfES Publications. Available at: http://dera.ioe.ac.uk/5551/2/report.pdf [Accessed: 31 August 2018].

Rowe, E. and Perry, L. B. (2020a) 'Inequalities in the private funding of public schools: parent financial contributions and school socioeconomic status', *Journal of Educational Administration and History*, 52(1): 42–59.

Rowe, E. and Perry, L. B. (2020b) 'Private financing in urban public schools: inequalities in a stratified education marketplace', *The Australian Educational Researcher*, 47(1): 19–37.

Rowe, J., Neale, I. and Perryfrost, L. (2019) *Exploring the Issue of Off-Rolling.* London: Ofsted. Available at: www.gov.uk/government/publications/off-rolling-exploring-the-issue [Accessed: 3 March 2020].

Sadler, K., Vizard, T., Ford, T., Goodman, R., Goodman, A. and MacManus,S. (2018) *Mental Health of Children and Young People in England, 2017: Trends and Characteristics.* NHS Digital, [online]. Available at: https://files.digital.nhs.uk/A0/273EE3/MHCYP%202017%20Trends%20Characteristics.pdf [Accessed: 18 January 2020].

Sahlberg, P. (2012) *Finnish Lessons: What Can the World Learn from Educational Change in Finland?* New York, NY: Teachers College Press.

Sahlberg, P. (2015) *Finnish Lessons 2.0: What can the World Learn from Educational Change in Finland?* 2nd edn. New York, NY: Teachers College Press.

Salokangas, M. and Ainscow, M. (2018) *Inside the Autonomous School: Making Sense of a Global Educational Trend*. London and New York, NY: Routledge.

Schnepf, S. V. and Volante, L. (2018) 'PISA and the future of global educational governance', in L. Volante (ed.) *The PISA Effect on Global Educational Governance*. New York, NY: Routledge, pp 217–25. doi: 10.4324/9781315440521.

Sellar, S. (2017) 'Making network markets in education: the development of data infrastructure in Australian schooling', *Globalisation, Societies and Education*, 15(3): 341–51.

Senate Employment, Education and Training References Committee (1988) *A Class Act: Inquiry into the Status of the Teaching Profession*. Canberra: Australian Government, Commonwealth of Australia. Available at: https://nla.gov.au/nla.obj-1665628206/view?partId=nla.obj-1671187660#page/n4/mode/1up

Senate Employment, Education and Training References Committee (2010) *Administration and reporting of NAPLAN testing*. Canberra: Australian Government, Commonwealth of Australia. Available at: http://www.aph.gov.au/Senate/committee/eet_ctte/naplan/report/report.pdf

Senate Employment, Education and Training References Committee (2014) *Effectiveness of the National Assessment Program – Literacy and Numeracy Final report*. Canberra: Australian Government, Commonwealth of Australia. Available at: https://www.aph.gov.au/parliamentary_business/committees/senate/education_and_employment/naplan13/report/index

Shaw, B., Menzies, L., Bernardes, E., Barrs, A., Nye, P. and Allen, R. (2016) *Ethnicity, Gender and Social Mobility*. London: Social Mobility Commission.

Shergold, P. (2020) *Looking to the Future: Report of the Review of Senior Secondary Pathways into Work, Further Education and Training*. Canberra: Education Services Australia.

Sila, U. and Dugain, V. (2019a) *Income Poverty in Australia: Evidence from the HILDA Survey*. Paris: OECD. Available at: https://doi.org/10.1787/322390bf-en

Sila, U. and Dugain, V. (2019b) *Income, Wealth and Earnings Inequality in Australia: Evidence from the HILDA Survey*. Paris: OECD. Available at: https://doi.org/10.1787/cab6789d-en.

Simpson, A. (2017) 'The misdirection of public policy: comparing and combining standardised effect sizes', *Journal of Education Policy*, 32(4): 450–66.

Simpson, A. (2018) 'Princesses are bigger than elephants: effect size as a category error in evidence-based education', *British Educational Research Journal*, 44(5): 897–913.

Sizmur, J., Ager, R., Bradshaw, J., Classick, R., Galvis, M., Packer, J., Thomas, D. and Wheater, R. (2019) *Achievement of 15-year-olds in England: PISA 2018 Results*. Slough: NFER.

Skattebol, J. and Hayes, D. (2016) 'Cracking with affect: relationality in young people's movements in and out of mainstream schooling', *Critical Studies in Education*, 57(1): 6–20.

Skattebol, J., Hill, T., Griffiths, A. and Wong, M. (2015) *Unpacking Youth Unemployment Final Report*. Sydney: Social Policy Research Centre, University of New South Wales.

Skattebol, J., Saunders, P., Redmond, G. and Cass, B. (2012) *Making a Difference: Building on Young People's Experiences of Economic Adversity: Final Report*. Sydney: Social Policy Research Centre, University of New South Wales.

Smith, L. and Todd, L. (2016) *Poverty Proofing the School Day: Evaluation and Development Report*. Newcastle upon Tyne: Research Centre for Teaching and Learning, Newcastle University.

Spielman, A. (2017) 'Enriching the fabric of education', Amanda Spielman's speech at the Festival of Education, GOV. UK, [online] 23 June. Available at: www.gov.uk/government/speeches/amanda-spielmans-speech-at-the-festival-of-education.

Spielman, A. (2018) Letter to Meg Hillier MP, Chair, Public Accounts Committee, House of Commons, Westminster, London.

Spina, N. (2019) '"Once upon a time": examining ability grouping and differentiation practices in cultures of evidence-based decision-making', *Cambridge Journal of Education*, 49(3): 329–48.

Stevenson, H. (2007) 'Restructuring teachers' work and trade union responses in England: bargaining for change?', *American Educational Research Journal*, 44(2): 224–51.

Stiglitz, J. E. (2013) *The Price of Inequality*. London: Penguin Books.

Stobart, G. and Eggen, T. (2012) 'High-stakes testing – value, fairness and consequences', *Assessment in Education: Principles, Policy & Practice*, 19(1): 1–6.

Stuff (2017) 'National Standards have officially ended in primary schools across the country', Stuff, [online] 12 December. Available at: www.stuff.co.nz/national/education/99774465/national-standards-have-officially-ended-in-primary-schools-across-the-country [Accessed: 28 October 2020].

Syal, R. (2014) 'Revealed: taxpayer-funded academies paying millions to private firms', *The Guardian*, [online] 12 January. Available at: www.theguardian.com/education/2014/jan/12/taxpayer-funded-academy-paying-millions-private-firms-schools-education-revealed-education [Accessed: 4 May 2020].

Tan, C. and Reyes, V. (2018) 'Shanghai-China and the emergence of a global reference society', in L. Volante (ed.) *The PISA Effect on Global Educational Governance*. New York, NY: Routledge, pp 61–76.

Teacher Workload Advisory Group (2018) *Making Data Work: Report of the Teacher Workload Advisory Group*. London: DfE. Available at: www.gov.uk/government/publications/teacher-workload-advisory-group-report-and-government-response [Accessed: 3 January 2019].

Teese, R. (2000) *Academic Success and Social Power: Examinations and Inequality*. Melbourne: Melbourne University Press.

Teese, R. and Polesel, J. (2003) *Undemocratic Schooling: Equity and Quality in Mass Secondary Education in Australia*. Melbourne: Melbourne University Press.

Tehan, D. (2019) 'Bringing phonics into Australian schools', Media Release, Ministers' Media Centre, Department of Education, Skills and Employment, [online] 15 October. Available at: https://ministers.dese.gov.au/tehan/bringing-phonics-australian-schools [Accessed: 25 July 2020].

The Children's Society (2018) *The Good Childhood Report 2018: Summary*. London: The Children's Society. Available at: www.basw.co.uk/resources/good-childhood-report-2018-summary [Accessed: 18 January 2020].

The Sutton Trust (2019) 'Private tuition polling 2019', The Sutton Trust, [online]. Available at: www.suttontrust.com/wp-content/uploads/2019/12/PrivateTuition2019-PollingTables.pdf [Accessed: 1 July 2020].

The Sutton Trust and the Social Mobility Commission (2019) *Elitist Britain 2019: The Educational Backgrounds of Britain's Leading People.* London: The Sutton Trust. Available at: www.suttontrust.com/wp-content/uploads/2019/12/Elitist-Britain-2019.pdf [Accessed: 11 May 2020].

Thinley P. (2016) 'Overview and "Heart Essence" of the Bhutanese Education System', in M. Schuelka and T. Maxwell (eds) *Education in Bhutan.* Springer, Singapore, pp 19–37. Available at: https://doi.org/10.1007/978-981-10-1649-3_2

Thomas, S. (2005) 'Taking teachers out of the equation: constructions of teachers in education policy documents over a ten-year period', *The Australian Educational Researcher*, 32(3): 45–62.

Thompson, G. (2013) 'NAPLAN, MySchool and accountability: teacher perceptions of the effects of testing', *The International Education Journal: Comparative Perspectives*, 12(2): 62–84.

Thompson, G., Hogan, A. and Rahimi, M. (2019) 'Private funding in Australian public schools: a problem of equity', *The Australian Educational Researcher*, 46(5): 893–910.

Thomson, P. (2002) *Schooling the Rustbelt Kids: Making the Difference in Changing Times.* Stoke-on-Trent and Sterling, VA: Trentham Books.

Thomson, P. (2007) 'Making education more equitable' in R. Teese, S. Lamb, M. Duru-Bellat and S. Helme (eds) *International Studies in Educational Inequality, Theory and Policy.* Dordrecht: Springer Netherlands, pp 905–22.

Thomson, S. and Lupton, R. (2017) *The Effects of English School System Reforms (2002–2014) on Pupil Sorting and Social Segregation: A Greater Manchester Case Study.* SPCC Working Paper 24. London: Centre for Analysis of Social Exclusion, LSE.

Thomson, S., De Bortoli, L., Nicholas, M., Hillman, K. and Buckley, S. (2010) *PISA in Brief: Highlights from the Full Australian Report. Challenges for Australian education: Results from PISA 2009.* Melbourne: Australian Council for Education Research.

Thomson, S., De Bortoli, S. and Buckley, S. (2019) *PISA in Brief 1: Student Performance.* Melbourne: Australian Council for Educational Research.

Thrupp, M. (1999) *Schools Making a Difference: Lets Be Realistic!* 1st edn. Buckingham and Philadelphia, PA: Open University Press.

Thrupp, M. (2018) 'The impact of the Kiwi standards', in M. Thrupp (ed.) *The Search for Better Educational Standards.* Cham: Springer, pp 157–80.

Tooley, J. and Darby, D. (1998) *Educational Research: A Critique. A Survey of Published Educational Research.* London: Ofsted.

Torgerson, C., Brooks, G. and Hall, J. (2006) *A Systematic Review of the Research Literature on the Use of Phonics in the Teaching of Reading and Spelling.* Nottingham: DfES Publications.

Treanor, M. (2018) 'Falling through the cracks: the cost of the school day for families living in in-work and out-of-work poverty', *Scottish Affairs,* 27(4): 486–511.

Tymms, P. (2004) 'Are standards rising in English primary schools?', *British Educational Research Journal,* 30(4): 477–94.

UK2070 Commission (2020) *Make No Little Plans: Acting at Scale for a Fairer and Stronger Future. Final Report of the UK2070 Commission.* Sheffield: UK2070 Commission. Available at: http://uk2070.org.uk/wp-content/uploads/2020/02/UK2070-FINAL-REPORT.pdf [Accessed: 17 July 2020].

UNESCO (United Nations Educational Scientific and Cultural Organisation) (2020) 'Government expenditure on primary, secondary and all education as a percentage of GDP 1975-2016' [online]. Available at http://data.uis.unesco.org [Accessed: 19 March 2020]

UNHCR (The UN Refugee Agency) (2020) *Figures at a Glance,* 18 June. Available at https://www.unhcr.org/en-au/figures-at-a-glance.html

UNICEF (United Nations International Children's Emergency Fund) (1992) *The United Nations Convention on the Rights of the Child*. London: UNICEF UK Available at: www.unicef.org. uk/wp-content/uploads/2016/08/unicef-convention-rights-child-uncrc.pdf [Accessed: 27 January 2020].

United Nations (2015) 'Ensure inclusive and equitable quality education and promote lifelong learning opportunities for all', Sustainable Development Goal 4, UN, [online]. Available at: https://sdgs.un.org/goals/goal4 [Accessed: 27 January 2020].

Valenzuela, J. P. and Montecinos, C. (2017) 'Structural reforms and equity in Chilean schools', in *Oxford Research Encyclopedia of Education*, [online], Oxford University Press USA.

Victoria, Directorate of School Education (1993) *Schools of the future: preliminary paper*. Melbourne: Directorate of School Education.

Vincent, C., Braun, A. and Ball, S. J. (2010) 'Local links, local knowledge: choosing care settings and schools', *British Educational Research Journal*, 36(2): 279–98.

Walker, M., Sainsbury, M., Worth, J., Bamforth, H. and Betts, H. (2015) *Phonics Screening Check Evaluation: Final Report*. London: DfE. Available at: www.nfer.ac.uk/publications/YOPC03/YOPC03.pdf [Accessed: 31 August 2018].

Waslander, S., Pater, C. and van der Weide, M. (2010) *Markets in Education: An Analytical Review of Empirical Research on Market Mechanisms in Education*. OECD Education Working Paper No 52. Paris: OECD Publishing. Available at: www.oecd-ilibrary.org/education/markets-in-education_5km4pskmkr27-en

Weale, S. (2018) '"An education arms race": inside the ultra-competitive world of private tutoring', *The Guardian*, [online] 12 May. Available at: www.theguardian.com/education/2018/dec/05/an-education-arms-race-inside-the-ultra-competitive-world-of-private-tutoring [Accessed: 1 July 2020].

Weale, S. (2020) 'Schools "converting toilet blocks into isolation booths"', *The Guardian*, [online] 18 January. Available at: https://www.theguardian.com/education/2020/jan/17/schools-converting-toilet-blocks-into-isolation-booths

Weldon, P. (2018) 'Early career teacher attrition in Australia: evidence, definition, classification and measurement', *Australian Journal of Education*, 62(1): 61–78.

Welsh Government (2014) *Qualified for Life. An Education Improvement Plan for 3 to 19-year-olds in Wales*. Cardiff: Department for Education and Skills, Welsh Government. Available at: https://dera.ioe.ac.uk/21054/1/141001-qualified-for-life-en_Redacted.pdf

Wheldall, K., Bell, N., Wheldall, R., Madelaine, A. and Reynolds, M. (2019) 'Performance of Australian children on the English Phonics Screening Check following systematic synthetic phonics instruction in the first two years of schooling', *Australian Journal of Learning Difficulties*, 24(2): 131–45.

White, S. (2019) 'Recruiting, retaining and supporting early career teachers for rural schools', in A. Sullivan, B. Johnson and M. Simons (eds) *Attracting and Keeping the Best Teachers: Issues and Opportunities*. Singapore: Springer Singapore, pp 143–59. doi: 10.1007/978-981-13-8621-3_8.

Whittaker, F. (2016) 'May: new grammar schools will help create "true meritocracy"', *Schools Week*, [online] 9 September. Available at: https://schoolsweek.co.uk/may-new-grammar-schools-will-help-create-true-meritocracy [Accessed: 29 July 2020].

Whitty, G. (2000) 'Teacher professionalism in new times', *Journal of In-Service Education*, 26(2): 281–95.

Wilkinson, R. G. and Pickett, K. (2009) *The Spirit Level: Why More Equal Societies Almost Always Do Better*. 1st edn. London: Allen Lane.

Wilson, J. (2011) *Are England's Academies More Inclusive or More 'Exclusive'? The Impact of Institutional Change on the Pupil Profile of Schools*. CEE Discussion Papers 0125. London: Centre for the Economics of Education, LSE. Available at: https://ideas.repec.org/p/cep/ceedps/0125.html [Accessed: 24 June 2020].

Windle, J. (2014) 'The rise of school choice in education funding reform: an analysis of two policy moments', *Educational Policy*, 28(2): 306–24.

Wolfram, C. (2020) *The Math(s) Fix: An Education Blueprint of the AI Age*. Champaign: Wolfram Media Inc.

Wrigley, T. (2014) *The Politics of Curriculum in Schools*. Policy Paper. London: Centre for Labour and Social Studies. Available at: http://classonline.org.uk/docs/2014_Policy_Paper_-_The_politics_of_curriculum_in_schools.pdf [Accessed: 11 May 2020].

Wrigley, T. (2018) 'Poor children need rich teaching not deficit labelling', in S. Gannon, R. Hattam and W. Sawyer (eds) *Resisting Educational Inequality: Reframing Policy and Practice in Schools Serving Vulnerable Communities*. Abingdon and New York, NY: Routledge, pp 266–74.

Wu, M. (2010) 'Measurement, sampling, and equating errors in largescale assessments', *Educational Measurement: Issues and Practice*, 29(4): 15–27.

Wu, M. (2016) 'What national testing data can tell us', in B. Lingard, G. Thompson and S. Sellar (eds) *National Testing in Schools: An Australian Assessment*. London and New York, NY: Routledge.

Wyn, J., Turnbull, M. and Grimshaw, L. (2014) *The Experience of Education: The Impacts of High Stakes Testing on School Students and their Families: A Qualitative Study*. Sydney: Whitlam Institute, University of Western Sydney.

Wyse, D. (2003) 'The national literacy strategy: a critical review of empirical evidence', *British Educational Research Journal*, 29(6): 903–16.

Wyse, D. and Goswami, U. (2008) 'Synthetic phonics and the teaching of reading', *British Educational Research Journal*, 34(6): 691–710.

Wyse, D. and Styles, M. (2007) 'Synthetic phonics and the teaching of reading: the debate surrounding England's "Rose Report"', *Literacy*, 41(1): 35–42.

Wyse, D. and Torrance, H. (2009) 'The development and consequences of national curriculum assessment for primary education in England', *Educational Research*, 51(2): 213–28.

Yates, L., Collins, C. and O'Connor, K. (2011) *Australia's Curriculum Dilemmas: State Cultures and the Big Issues*. Melbourne: Melbourne University Publishing.

Young, M. (2013) 'Overcoming the crisis in curriculum theory: a knowledge-based approach', *Journal of Curriculum Studies*, 45(2): 101–18.

Index

Note: Page numbers for tables appear in italics.